# Beyond Book Buddies

# Beyond Book Buddies

*Interdisciplinary Teaching Across the Grades*

Jeanne Guthrie
Karen M. Perea

CORWIN PRESS, INC.
A Sage Publications Company
Thousand Oaks, California

*For information address:*

Corwin Press, Inc.
A Sage Publications Company
2455 Teller Road
Thousand Oaks, California 91320

SAGE Publications Ltd.
6 Bonhill Street
London EC2A 4PU
United Kingdom

SAGE Publications India Pvt. Ltd.
M-32 Market
Greater Kailash I
New Delhi 110 048 India

Printed in the United States of America

**Library of Congress Cataloging-in-Publication Data**

Guthrie, Jeanne, 1941–
    Beyond book buddies: Interdisciplinary teaching across the grades  /
Jeanne Guthrie, Karen M. Perea.
        p.  cm.
    Includes bibliographical references and index.
    ISBN 0-8039-6287-8 (pbk.  :  alk. paper)
    1. Elementary school teaching—United States.
    2. Interdisciplinary approach in education—United States.
    3. Constructivism (Education) United States.  4. Nongraded schools—
United States.  5. Education, Elementary—Activity programs—United
States.  I. Perea, Karen M., 1956–  .  II. Title.
    LB1555.G88   1995
    372.11′02—dc20                                         95-7749

This book is printed on acid-free paper.

95  96  97  98  99  10  9  8  7  6  5  4  3  2  1

Corwin Press Production Editor:  Diane S. Foster
Typesetter:  Janelle LeMaster

# Contents

# Foreword

*Beyond Book Buddies* presents several important themes in the professional practice of its authors and in the art of teaching in America at the end of the 20th century. The authors have become teachers-as-researchers and reflective practitioners to elevate their knowledge, experience, and fine teaching skills to a level of systematic research-based practice that matches theory with daily life in real classrooms. They are developers and users of knowledge. The themes of their work also elevate this book beyond a description of classroom methods to a representation of the power of new possibilities in our profession. Elementary teachers will naturally find value in the book, but administrators and curriculum and program developers will also appreciate its contribution to operationalizing theory.

One important theme that this book represents is the synthesis of several important current teaching strategies into an integrated plan. We know that such a plan, with strategies that conceptually match the plan, is critical to increasing student achievement. This plan is founded upon constructivist theory. The best elements of cooperative learning, cross-grade grouping, peer teaching, whole language practices, thematic teaching and integrated curriculum, performance-based curriculum, and authentic assessment come together to form a new, exciting whole. Learning is an integrative process, and this is an integrative model.

*Beyond Book Buddies* brings a very wide spectrum of important, broad-based concepts and skills in content areas into focus, but it moves beyond that focus into integrating the attitudes, dispositions, and skills of areas such as research, higher-level thinking, a variety of problem-solving opportunities, responsibility to others and to society, conflict resolution, working productively with others, social interaction, appreciation of the arts, multicultural learning, historical perspective, personal health, and appreciation of diverse talents and abilities. The adult and business world is asking that we send students to it with knowledge and skills such as these.

Another theme that underlies the authors' work is the clear message that we must *begin* to teach with the *end* in mind. Regardless of other messages that may be portrayed, this is the pure essence of the standards-based education movement. These teachers base their daily instruction on distinct statements of what they want their students to know and be able to do after many days of instruction have passed. They model the belief that every child can set learning goals, develop a plan to meet those goals, use self and peer evaluation, and meet performance standards, as long as proper and sufficient instructional support is provided. An important part of that support can be provided by other children.

No person who chooses to read this book will be unaware of the tremendous challenges today's teachers face as the social, economic, and political forces of our society bear upon our families and children and affect our classrooms. Teaching is a profession that, by its structure, often forces its practitioners into dealing with those challenges in isolation from each other. A final distinctive feature or theme represented by this book is a view of practitioners who counter the isolation of teaching with systematic collaborative daily practice. They also face many challenges, but they have chosen to concentrate on the possibilities of their opportunity to directly influence 40 or 50 children for a whole school year. There is extraordinary power in the combined expertise, creativity, and energy of teachers, and we can trust that power to foster change. Collaborative practice, coupled with a philosophy of opportunity rather than defeat, is a key to improving education from inside the classroom.

Educators in America are increasingly exploring the meaning of the future of our education system in a democratic society as we move into a new century. There are many implications of such a system, but inherent in it is the concept of community in the school and classroom. This book is future oriented in its themes and teaching units. It speaks to collaborative support for teachers, but, even more important, it speaks to teaching concepts of community and to collaborative support for all learners.

Pamela Hopkins
Director, Elementary Education
School District 2
Colorado Springs, Colorado

# Preface

---

*Beyond Book Buddies* introduces teachers and students to the delights of cross-grade-level learning. Students of both primary and intermediate grades are able to interact together in an authentic task that is an extension of a shared outcome. While having fun, students are reinforcing skills that they will need to be successful in the future. At the same time they are reaching out of the classroom and into the community to bring the real world into education.

The Introduction states how the ideas for the book came into being, the basis for instruction in the constructivist theory, how to get started with cross-grade-level lessons, how to select units of study, and the philosophies upon which the book was written. The outcomes established by the Harrison School District of Colorado Springs are also presented. These outcomes are the standards on which the performance-based assessments were developed.

Connection 1 of the book begins students on a journey into the world of research, the basis for all independent learning. It is quite amazing that once students are exposed to the process, even first graders begin to look to multi-resources for information.

Connection 2 captures students' imagination by first studying the moon and then creating an original moon colony on which they might one day live. Students must work not only with their buddy but with other buddy pairs to create a harmonious but survivable place to live in the future.

In Connection 3, students use math manipulatives to create new math games that the buddy pairs can share. They must write readable directions, teach the game, and analyze the game for its higher-level mathematical thinking concepts.

Connection 4 invites students' participation in a mail system that not only teaches them responsibility and organization but allows them to provide a service for the entire school.

Connection 5 gives students the opportunity to go out into their community to become aware of their environment and what they will need to do in the future to protect it. This task brings parents and the business community into an awareness of ecology seen through the eyes of the children who will inherit our Earth.

Connection 6 challenges students to study the inventions that have evolved through the years to give them the lifestyle to which they are accustomed. It also asks them to look to the future to create other inventions based on needs and future needs. Budding scientists will blossom during this activity!

In Connection 7, students have the opportunity to bring the arts to the forefront. While those living in larger communities have the chance to visit local museums to see the great works of the past and the changing techniques of the present and future, many students living in smaller cities and towns do not. This task makes students aware that art consists of many things, from folk art to architecture to modern graphics.

Connection 8 gives students the awareness of the importance of each day in their lives. It also helps them become aware of the cultural diversity of Americans by challenging them to learn of special holidays celebrated by a variety of Americans, especially those of "new" citizens who have come to be a part of our country. Finally, the task gives students a memory from the year that will be meaningful now and in the future.

The task in Connection 9 encourages students to study the past and, at the same time, bring it into the present by creating a special room for a classroom museum. The task also becomes a model for any other special areas that students would like to create.

Creating a neighborhood newspaper, the task in Connection 10, brings students into communication with the student body and the members of the community around their school. It encourages students to use the interview process to find articles of interest, and it sets a standard for which students can reach.

Today, we know that a healthy diet and an exercise program are necessary for a healthy life. The task in Connection 11 uses the constructivist process to enable students to create menus and exercises for the benefit of the entire family. It makes them aware of the need for developing healthy habits at an early age.

Finally, in Connection 12, students are asked to set a standard of excellence by becoming publishers for the works of other boys and girls in the school. Students will use editing, interviewing, illustrating, and binding skills to produce the stories and books of their schoolmates.

In writing *Beyond Book Buddies* we wanted to share the fun, excitement, and success found in our teaching experience. Our lessons have made learning and teaching exciting for both our students and ourselves. We have learned the importance of authentic tasks that give students the responsibility for learning. We have discovered the importance of using rubrics to let students know, before assessment, the standards that have been set for optimum performance. We have reinforced our understanding and belief that all children can meet those standards given the opportunity and support. As teachers, we now have become facilitators.

Our approach has also created a family feeling between our two classrooms. As our ideas have spread to other classrooms, the school has become a community that illuminates respect and caring. We equate ourselves to the old woman who lived in a shoe—many children interacting, learning, sharing, and living together, even if the noise level is somewhat elevated and the area in the shoe is a little crowded at times. Buddies helping buddies learn. What could be better?

## Acknowledgments

We would like to express our gratitude to our colleagues, friends, and families who have been supportive of us as we persevered to bring this book to completion.

The administrators of Harrison School District 2 in Colorado Springs, Colorado, have been our inspiration in the development of *Beyond Book Buddies*. We owe much to Tony Stansberry, Superintendent of the Harrison School District; Hal Terry, former Superintendent; Pam Hopkins, Director of Elementary Education; Bill O'Rourke, Director of Secondary Education; Kay Cushing, Coordinator of Research and Evaluation; Chris Czajka, Coordinator of Staff Development; and a special thank-you to Richard Disario, Supervisor of District Media Services.

We especially thank Lee Cope, Principal of Otero Elementary, who encouraged us to experiment in cross-grade-level activities even when it meant extra noise and confusion. It was she who authorized us to have a connecting door and easy access to each other, thus making the perfect situation for our cross-grade-level connections.

Our fellow teachers and friends deserve our special gratitude for sharing their ideas, lending us their support, and encouraging us every step of the way. We owe much to the staff of Otero.

To our husbands and children we owe our love and gratitude for their constant cheers and support over the past 4 years. We thank Mark Perea, for without his assistance our book would never have been completed in its final form; he has been our computer teacher and all-round consultant on everything technical, patiently correcting our errors and showing us how to use the computer. David Guthrie's organization and perseverance enabled completion of the hundreds of little chores that needed to be done during the publishing process; without him, manuscripts would never have been copied and mailed. To our children, Staci Perea, Dave, Ellen, Scott, and Troy Guthrie, R. Scott Guthrie, and Laure, Joe, and Jessica Pilgrim we owe the reason for writing the book. They are living proof that the standards we adhere to work! We see the results every day!

Jeanne Guthrie
Karen M. Perea

# Introduction:
# Beyond Book Buddies

The ideas presented in *Beyond Book Buddies* began with the decision to let our fifth-grade students read with our first graders several times a month. The results were satisfying; younger students loved the stories, and fifth graders had a legitimate reason for practicing oral reading skills. As teachers, we were able to "oohh" and "ahh" and solve the occasional spat that occurs naturally when 50 children are scattered about one classroom in chairs, rockers, bean bags, and pillows crammed into every nook and cranny.

We were pleased with our program, and as the year progressed, the first graders even began to read to their fifth-grade buddies. The older children patted themselves on the back for the miracle they had achieved in teaching their little friends how to read! We were inspired, so little by little we added holiday activities: a feast of nations, dying eggs, and so on. Again, as teachers we beamed brightly at the success of our program.

One problem did keep recurring. Having 50 children in one room began to raise our anxiety level. We "hung in there" for the great good we were providing for our students. (We later learned that everyone appreciated our activities except for the teacher in the adjoining room, who was gracious enough to shut her door when she saw us congregating together!) The boys and girls were happy, parents thought that buddies were adorable, and there was definitely a feeling of friendship when the children passed in the halls or played in the schoolyard. Other classes were even starting to follow our example. What pride we felt! We had really inspired a book buddy program in our school.

It wasn't until the following year that we began to think "What if . . . ?" Both of us, believing in whole language, began to wonder if our two classes might be able to write a story together to extend the activities we were using in each individual classroom. We decided to test the statement "If you want to really learn something, teach it!"

Buddy writing began with some success but did not achieve the wonderful results that we had envisioned. Assessment of our attempts quickly brought us to the conclusion that there was no way we would see "budding authors" with so many pairs trying to talk louder than each other (and succeeding in many cases!). We decided to divide the students into two groups composed of half first graders and half fifth graders. This arrangement was a definite improvement noisewise (the teacher one room over was even able to leave her door open!), but it still wasn't what we'd hoped for. We felt our students could be learning at the same time they were bonding together, so we went back to our drawing board. We both agreed that more planning and modeling on our part was needed. Too often, our students didn't know the purpose of the activity. How could we solve this problem? At this point *Beyond Book Buddies* began to take form.

We decided to start with the outcomes we wanted our students to achieve. We used those adapted by the Harrison School District of Colorado Springs, but any approved goals or outcomes could be used.

We felt that themes would help us achieve our outcomes. We wanted to include performance-based assessments so we could see the results of our program. Our challenge was to find relevant materials and activities that included all that we felt was necessary to ensure that learning took place for all our students.

As we began to write and try our units, we finally saw some of the results we had been hoping for. Each year, we have experimented, revised, and reintroduced the units now found in our book. We don't pretend that everything has always worked with every child, but we feel that the learning and the bonding have created enthusiasm for school and helped students develop a desire for lifelong learning.

Teachers looking for alternative and innovative ways to inspire their students should find our book of interest. We have selected universal outcomes involving interdisciplinary themes and have followed the latest in educational research. *Beyond Book Buddies* is based on what we know of whole language, cooperative learning, cross-grade-level peer tutoring, performance-based assessment, thematic topics, and the constructivist theory. Teachers are free to use our book as a beginning, adapting the ideas to their own students' interests and grade levels.

We decided to share our experiences because we have seen the growth in our classes throughout the five years we have spent developing this book. We feel our approach to learning is fun, promotes a feeling of family in the school, and helps children develop the skills they will need to compete in our ever growing and complex society.

The Council of Chief State School Officers has stated that we must challenge ourselves to create new partnerships and shared responsibilities for children's development. We agree.

## Terminology

*Beyond Book Buddies* contains several specifically chosen terms that require definition and explanation.

Our units are called *Connections* because we believe in interdisciplinary themes that integrate content with reading and writing processes across the disciplines. We believe that reading and writing are abilities deeply rooted in the development of oral language, listening, and speaking. Our Connections focus on themes of life, society, values, and academic knowledge.

Our lessons are called *Cycles* because we believe that learning is cyclical. Each Cycle provides students opportunities to build upon existing knowledge, gain new meaning, promote higher-level thinking, and experience the joy of working to help others. As the Cycle is repeated throughout the various Connections, the children are able to capitalize on natural interests and are given the opportunity to work in large groups, small groups, and buddy pairs, all of which link them together both socially and academically. We believe that the variety of interactions provided enables our children to bond during the year. Older and younger students learn together and come to an appreciation of each other, often providing support in unusual places.

Finally, assessments are called *analysis and reflection* (or *rubrics* for short) because students come to us with different strengths, abilities, and weaknesses. All of these need to be addressed individually. Performance-based assessment helps us meet those individuals' needs by setting a standard and allowing us to help the child meet that standard. Conferencing allows students the opportunity to self-analyze and gives them time for the reflection that is necessary for a child to take control of learning.

## Components

Each Connection contains the following components in the three Cycles labeled Primary, Intermediate, and Bonding:

- Interdisciplinary theme
- Outcomes to be achieved
- Materials for implementation
- Student task
- Teaching suggestions
- Analysis and reflection
- Suggested book lists

## Rationale for *Beyond Book Buddies*

Robert Helliard of the U.S. Federal Communications Commission has stated that the rate at which knowledge is growing is such that when a child born today graduates from college the amount of knowledge in the world will have increased fourfold, that by the time that child is 50 the amount will be 32 times as great, and that 97% of everything known in the world will have been learned since that child's birth.

What does this mean for children? It means that the tools students will need for the 21st century are the abilities to think critically, to adapt to change, and to be lifelong learners. America has shifted from a manufacturing-to an information-based economy. Technology is important, and the rate of change and knowledge is escalating. Also, because of our increasing global interdependence, students will need communication skills to speak in other languages, to relate interpersonally, and to survive in a context of multicultural diversity.

If the purpose of education is to maximize all students' learning so that they can function in society, then students must possess the skills, attitudes, and abilities to maximize their option both in school and in adulthood.

As school districts move away from strictly information-centered curriculum to the inclusion of higher-level thinking skills and processes, there will be changes and new terminology with which you, as teachers, should be familiar.

All of the Cycles and Connections in our book are based on the constructivist theory of learning and acquiring knowledge. We have chosen this course of action because, from experience, we know it works, and because we believe that teachers should encourage students to actively form questions and seek the answers to those questions rather than passively waiting for the teacher or the textbook to tell them what is important. We have seen the high interest level, the desire to work, and the improved behavior as students become involved in activities.

We feel that students should be able to use all resources available as they seek answers to their questions. One resource cannot possibly provide all the latest or most complete information. Students should be encouraged to seek information from multiple books, magazines, brochures, videos, reference books, interviews, or any other materials. If manipulative or physical materials are available, we feel that these, too, should be given to the children to provide yet another means of acquiring knowledge.

We also feel that students should be challenged to use higher-level thinking skills as they explore content. They should be encouraged to classify, analyze, predict, and create. Whether in the Primary, Intermediate, or Bonding Cycle, we have attempted to provide opportunities for students to rise above the literal and challenge them to create the original. This includes using their prior knowledge and that of others to build concepts. As they formulate questions, search for answers, construct meaning, and create new situations to test their ideas, they find an entire world of learning that stretches beyond the textbook or the lecture.

Another reason we have chosen the constructivist theory is that it encourages students to interact with one another. We feel that real learning occurs when students are able to formulate ideas, discuss them, and come to conclusions together. Combine that with peer coaching and both younger and older students benefit to the maximum.

The student activities in our book provide thoughtful, open-ended tasks for students to use as they begin to learn for themselves. They are broad in nature, yet give students the opportunity to elaborate on original thinking as they work to complete the tasks.

Within the concepts we have mentioned above, we still believe in modeling or demonstrating a task for students. Both of us have found real success in using *Easy* books to do this. Whether you want to demonstrate math, science, social studies, or story sense, you can find an *Easy* book to do so. The possibilities are limitless. One hour spent in the school library is all you'll need to find an example of whatever concept you need to model.

Don't feel that the intermediate students will be offended by your using *Easy* books. They are short and colorful and provide the examples or meanings you wish to demonstrate. In fact, many are quite complex. They also relieve you of having to read encyclopedia excerpts that mean nothing to the students and are certainly boring to you!

## Questions We're Asked

- *What are our children learning?*

This most frequently asked question involves the intermediate students. Parents want to be sure that the older students are not giving up time that could be spent learning the skills they will need for the future. It is generally accepted by the primary parents that their children benefit from the cross-grade-level peer teaching situation. However, intermediate parents want to know what their children are learning besides the obvious leadership skills. They want to be sure that the activities engaged in are challenging and not simply busy activities that take their children away from the academics they will need so much in the future. Our answer is that because we share a common outcome, set standards, and encourage the students to make choices and learn in a social situation, we are giving those in both classes the skills they will need. Most important, we know that no one can teach what he or she doesn't really know and understand completely.

- *How much time should we spend?*

One question asked by teachers and our principal when we first began was the amount of time spent in the bonding activities. When we are ready for a bonding activity, we set aside 30 minutes each day for our students to work together. Remember that the teaching of the original concept has already begun in each of the classrooms, and the bonding activity becomes review, practice, and the performance-based assessment. If there are special holiday activities, we allow 1 hour on Friday afternoons. These activities tend to be in the "fun" category. The daily half hour is quite adequate for our academic work. At times, we let individual big buddies work with little buddies. We have found this quite effective when younger students need individual help or need to focus on seat work. For the slower intermediate students, allowing them to help gives them a chance to practice reading orally and affords them a leadership role, thus building their self-esteem.

- *What is success?*

Of course, teachers want to know our level of success. Yes, we've had a few bombs, none of which are included in *Beyond Book Buddies*. We believe in the success of our cross-grade-level peer teaching because we've been able to experiment, revise, rewrite, and reject over the years we've worked together. We don't pretend to tell experienced teachers or new ones that everything works with every child, but we certainly feel that the balance is in favor of trying peer teaching.

- *How should children be paired?*

One of the more difficult questions we are asked is how we pair the younger child to the older child. To be honest, we have no criteria for making perfect pairs. We usually spend several sessions on the playground together observing the students and noting those who get along, allowing for a natural bonding to occur. We jot down those pairs who have connected. If necessary, we will combine students into buddy pairs. Like you, we are able to tell which combinations to avoid. However, there have been many successful pairs of active children of whom we initially had doubts. We firmly believe that if children are to learn to get along with others in this world, they need the exposure of working with many different personalities.

A problem occurs when classes are uneven. The way we have dealt with this is to put two little buddies with one big buddy if the primary class is larger. If the intermediate class is larger, then we pair two big buddies with a little buddy. The best way we have found to do this is to let one of the intermediate students of lesser ability work with a more academically prepared peer.

On the issue of student absences, we simply let the buddy decide if he or she would like to join another buddy pair or work alone. New students are either assigned as part of a new pair if there are uneven numbers or added to an existing pair.

We have, on occasion, encountered some students who cannot work together. In this instance, we will hold a conference with the students to determine the challenges they may be having with each other and try to come to some workable solutions. Our belief is that in today's society we need to learn to work with many people and that give and take is part of the process of learning to work together.

The question of keeping the same buddy continually arises. We have found that keeping the buddy pairs together for the entire year is most successful. One year we did try switching partners for each new Connection, but neither the older buddies or the younger buddies were pleased with the changes. The little buddies couldn't connect, and the big buddies had to reestablish rapport with each new boy or girl. It also was more comfortable to know the abilities of their little partner so that they could work with him or her more effectively.

## Getting Started

For those of you who would like to try cross-grade-level peer teaching, we offer these suggestions: First, find a teacher who is willing to experiment and learn with you. It is important that your philosophies of teaching are similar because you will be team teaching. Next, know the outcomes that your district expects from all of its students. If these aren't readily available, feel free to use those in our book. They are general and broad enough to encompass what most education departments require. Once you've decided on a common goal, brainstorm together how each of you will use the Connections in *Beyond Book Buddies* most effectively. We expect you to use our lessons as a core, but we encourage you to bring your own expertise into each one. When creating your student work pages, be sure to enhance them with pictures or graphics that will motivate your students. Finally, you have only to match your students and step out into the unknown. We assure you the anxiety is worth the results!

## Beginning

An effective beginning for the program is a field trip or playground experience that allows you to see how the different students interact with each other. Use a clipboard to note those who are especially cooperating or disagreeing. It will also be important to note those children who don't seem to be bonding with anyone, creating the necessity to select particularly outgoing buddies for these children.

After the shared experience, ask for input from each of the classes. It is good to do this in each classroom rather than in a mixed group so that honest feelings can be expressed without embarrassing anyone or having hurt feelings. Armed with the notes from the shared experience and the personal input, you will be able to make good buddy pairs.

## Proximity

It is convenient if the two classes are near each other but not necessary for a strong buddy program. Because you will each be taking half of each class, students quickly adjust to movement. In fact, we have found that they so look forward to the buddy experience that their behavior is easily controlled while moving from classroom to classroom.

## Bonding Together

If you want to create real bonding, take field trips together. One very productive outing is to the local nursing home. Before going, share stories about the elderly and be sure to address the physical conditions that some of the residents might be experiencing. Once these are explained, even the youngest students feel quite comfortable. It is very exciting to remember new friends on holidays, and the friends give real meaning to letter writing.

Another bonding activity is having lunch together. It would be wise to clear the event with the lunchroom and the principal, but especially in the first week, the older child will be of great assistance to the younger one who might be feeling a little nervous about being back in school. Eating together also keeps the lunch line moving and the floor clean!

## *Discussion*

After each class has had its lessons and a buddy time has been completed, it is necessary to go back to individual classrooms to discuss any problems or successes the students have had. It is at this sharing time that a lot of learning takes place. It's always humorous to find "the pot calling the kettle black." Even though we have modeled and explained how we want our students to handle various cooperative situations, especially those involving discipline, it is still necessary to talk together about something that was difficult for the buddy pairs. Again, this is just as important for the little buddies as it is for their older buddies. Bigger children can be intimidating to new first graders; these fears need to be addressed.

An example of the need to discuss cross-level activities is one that occurred to us. Intermediate students were criticizing a fellow classmate because her primary buddy wasn't reading or writing as well as some of the other little buddies. It was necessary to explain that we all have talents but that some of us learn more easily than others. With our discussion, the older buddies began to support that particular little buddy, helping their classmate instead of rebuking and blaming her.

## Performance-Based Assessment

As school districts across the nation develop outcomes and standards, there are several methods of assessing, or measuring, how well students have met those outcomes and how much they have learned: standardized tests (e.g., Iowa Basic Skills Test), portfolios, or performance-based assessments.

Performance-based assessments are based on real-world examples of excellence. All of us have experienced these kinds of tests when we have taken driving tests, tried out for sports teams or drama productions, or applied for a typing position, just to name a few. To achieve each of these outcomes, we had to prove we had the skills. Having just read about any of them wasn't enough. We had to be able to "do" them. Examples of such a task are being able to give change from a dollar and being able to write a proper business letter.

In performance-based assessments, students know up front what is required of them. The outcomes, tasks, and criteria are clearly established and drive the instruction. Teachers literally teach the test. Students are given models/examples, instructional support, and time to reflect and practice self-evaluation. Children learn as they perform.

Performance-based assessments have other advantages for students. They permit multiple means to get answers, involve mastering problems, couple skills and information with thought, and demand rehearsal. Performance-based assessments shift the role of student from passive observer to active learner and the teacher from lecturer to facilitator.

In the April 1990 issue of *Phi Beta Kappan*, Chester E. Finn, Jr. noted that education or learning is the result achieved only when the process has been effective. In other words, assessment becomes instruction. Performance-based assessment doesn't take time out from learning—it *is* learning!

There are many ways of finding the time to confer with each child after each activity. You will find the moments based on individual classroom schedules. Some suggested times are during silent reading, while others are completing seat work, or when the children are working. The important point is to find the time. You must! Nothing is more frustrating or less informative than an unexplained grade. Remember that C- college paper returned to you unmarked and without comment? Students can change if they know what needs to be changed.

Finally, enjoy your efforts. Some will be so successful that you won't believe it. Others might make you wonder what you're doing. Keep going! The children and the school will benefit by learning together and respecting each other. All efforts will be worth the results!

## *Activity Selection*

When you and a fellow teacher have made the decision to try cross-grade-level teaching, select a Connection that you feel will be beneficial for all of the students involved. Make plans to begin the Primary and Intermediate Cycles in individual classrooms prior to the planned buddy experience. Times for these grade-level activities will vary. Teach these cycles as you would teach any lesson—by modeling, monitoring independent work, and reviewing the concepts to be learned. When both classes are feeling comfortable with the development of their own Cycles, prepare the classes for the peer-tutoring task. In individual classrooms, explain what will be expected from each group, making sure that the older buddies are completely familiar with the rubric that will guide them, and that the younger buddies understand that they are as responsible for performance as their big buddies.

You will find that some of the buddy tasks are quite involved and will take the better part of the semester to complete. Therefore, it is suggested that you be selective in the Connections you choose.

## **Materials**

You will find that, other than books for research, very few materials are needed for each of the Connections. Paper and pencils are items that are available for most students, as are markers or crayons, scissors, and glue.

Tag board or chart paper will be helpful, but any large paper can be used. Other materials are the items all teachers save (tubes, odd boxes, egg cartons, etc.). The rest will be brought in by the students as they decide how they wish to expand on the tasks they are given.

Computers and computer programs enhance students' work. If they are available, we encourage their use. (If your students are like ours, they already know more about computers than you do!)

## Instructional Strategies

Teachers looking for alternative and innovative ways to inspire their students should find our book of interest. We have selected universal outcomes involving interdisciplinary themes, following the latest in educational research. *Beyond Book Buddies* is based on what we know of whole language, cooperative learning, cross-grade-level peer tutoring, and thematic topics. Teachers are free to use our book as a beginning, adapting the ideas to their own students' interests and grade levels.

We decided to share our experiences because we have seen the academic and social growth in our classes throughout the five years in which we developed *Beyond Book Buddies.* We feel our approach to learning is fun, promotes a feeling of family in the school, and helps children develop the skills that they will need to compete in our ever growing and complex society.

### *Whole Language*

First and foremost, it should be understood that whole language is not a practice but a philosophy, a belief, a set of intentions. It is with this in mind then that the structure of the classroom becomes authentic. There is little use of prepared materials to teach reading and writing, and more focus placed on literature and print that is used for appropriate purposes.

Research has shown that anyone using language is using all systems to make meaning and to accomplish a desired outcome. It is well known the world over that babies acquire language by using it, not by learning its separate parts. Reading, writing, and learning will make more sense to students if they are taught through real, authentic tasks rather than by drill and practice.

### *Cooperative Learning*

Cooperative learning is as old as mankind. A major contributor to the success of our species has been the ability to work cooperatively. By taking this philosophy of learning into the classroom we change the trend from the "me" classroom to the "we" classroom. The focus is then shifted from a competitive, individual environment to a "let's do it together" environment.

Cooperative learning goes beyond having students sitting side by side, discussing materials, helping others, and sharing information. As important as the aforementioned items are, cooperative learning is much more. Students begin to realize that they are interdependent on one another, but that individually they are accountable for a part of the material. Students learn to function in a heterogeneous group as they share leadership and responsibility for others. Students begin to develop social skills and become evaluators in their processing and effectiveness as a group.

### *Cross-Grade-Level Peer Tutoring*

Research has shown that cross-grade-level peer tutoring benefits primary students with an increase in time on task, listening for details, focusing on language, and decoding skills. Tutors make gains in attitudes toward school and in academic achievements when the activities are meaningful and built on prior knowledge.

We are in accordance with research that says there are several phases to cross-grade-level collaborating and that each phase is as important as the actual activity. The first phase is the preparation of the individual class activities that are related to the outcome to be achieved. The second phase is preparing each class for the buddy activity. The third phase is the actual cross-grade-level interaction, with individual expectations and responsibilities stated in the rubrics discussed with the children. The final phase is the sharing of the product with presentations and a recap of the events and the time together.

## *Thematic Topics*

We believe a thematic unit built around the children's interests is the whole language tool for making reading, writing, listening, and speaking meaningful.

A thematic unit should be more than a set of dittos that mentions a particular subject. Rather, it should show children how they interact with themselves and their environment. Thematic units give authentic reasons for literacy and working toward an integrated knowledge base.

## Standards

The goal of education today is to teach students the attitudes, problem-solving skills, and communication skills they will need when they leave public education to go on to college or enter a very competitive workforce.

Following the example of other industrialized nations like Germany, France, Australia, Britain, and Japan, both educational and political leaders in the United States have met to develop "standards" that will define academic excellence in preparing our students to become productive citizens.

Standards are defined by some people as banners, the signs that provide direction and framework for teachers and school districts as they develop curriculum and teach America's children. Standards become the benchmarks that tell to what degree or level students have learned.

Within the past few years, starting with former President Bush's summit with the governors in 1989, curriculum standards have been or are currently being established in various subject areas. These projects include, among others, the Standards Project for English Language Arts, the National Committee on Science Education and Assessment, and the Math Standards.

The state of Colorado has recently passed a bill requiring all districts to develop standards by the year 1994. The Harrison School District leads the state in the development of these standards. Since 1990, the district's administration and staff have researched and developed what we want our children to be able to do when they graduate from our system. The resulting outcomes are specific enough to provide guidance, yet broad enough to allow teachers and schools to adjust their curriculums to meet their individual strengths and talents (see Appendix A).

The ability of all students to be able to meet the standards might be a concern for teachers. If a child has difficulty in some area of performance, perhaps because of a disability, a teacher might feel that the meeting of standards is asking too much.

Realize that standards are the goals set for all students. By including every child in the expectation of achievement of those goals, standards are not lowered for any child. Instead, it is necessary to find whatever is needed to help every child meet goals. Technology, media, special personnel, and any other instructional materials will help the student achieve the outcomes that have been set.

High expectations bring lofty results. One cannot help but be reminded of the example of Stephen Hawking, who is considered to be one of the most brilliant theoretical physicists since Einstein. Although confined to a wheel-chair with a crippling disease, unable to speak clearly, and communicating with a pencil in his mouth and a computer, he has let his mind soar across the vastness of space and time to unlock the secrets of the universe. He has not let his disability prevent him from setting high standards. Instead, he has found the means of meeting those standards of performance and has made a great contribution to our world.

Standards allow us to integrate instruction and assessment, thereby fostering improved student performance. They allow students the means of becoming productive adults.

The key quality points of performance-based curriculum that support the Harrison School District outcomes are listed in Appendix B.

## Rubrics

By definition, a scoring rubric is a set of guidelines and indicators for assessing student work. A typical rubric contains a scale, states the dimensions to be assessed, and provides key traits for finding the place on the scale for a particular performance.

In everyday language this simply means that the rubric will be a student's level of achievement (Advanced, Proficient, Basic, or In Progress), what will be graded (correct letter format, spelling, etc.), and what constitutes an Advanced, Proficient, Basic, or In Progress score.

Also included in the rubric are the district outcome and the task to be performed. Students will know all of these criteria prior to performance. They will have before them a standard of excellence. They will know beforehand what constitutes a perfect performance. Teachers will provide models or examples for students along with the rubric.

Before rubrics are given to students, teachers will introduce the skills needed to perform the tasks. Children won't be asked, for example, to make a bibliography without having had lessons on correct form and being shown examples of bibliographies.

With rubrics come the opportunity for students to engage in learning with each other. They will be encouraged to share and discuss ways to meet the standards of excellence stated. They will edit together, rewrite together, and practice performances together.

When tasks have been performed and assessed, students will confer with the teacher to discuss strengths of the project and areas where improvement is needed. No more C- paper without an explanation!

The general rubrics for the Primary, Intermediate, and Bonding Cycles are found in "Resources" at the end of the book.

## Writing and Editing

To be literate, one must be able to write. Today, writing crosses the curriculum as a key element in every assessment.

While it is true that when writing we go in and out of the stages of writing, there is a general sequence for composition. The process begins with the brainstorming and listing of ideas. At this time, ideas can be categorized, expanded, or discarded. The actual writing begins after this prewriting activity. During this first draft, it is important to develop the message of the assignment before dealing with the spelling and punctuation errors. Editing is an important part of the writing process, but it would be inappropriate to focus on all of the mistakes during this initial writing phase. Too much criticism at this time will keep your students from taking learning risks for fear of making mistakes. They might also substitute known words instead of stretching vocabulary. "Nice," for instance, is much easier to spell than "beautiful."

Remember that we all make mistakes and your students are no different. Editing will help correct the spelling, punctuation, and grammatical errors that the first draft might yield.

Not all writing needs to be edited, however. Only those papers, stories, booklets, or poems selected to be read by an audience will be expected to be corrected to meet the standards of good English grammar. Other writings are merely discarded.

After editing, students will be expected to rewrite compositions. With your support and guidance they will learn the joy and importance of the written word.

# APPENDIX A

## Significant Student Outcomes

*Literacy*

- Reading: Construct meaning when reading in all subject areas for the purposes of becoming informed, performing a task, and enjoying literature
- Writing: Communicate in writing to multiple audiences for the purposes of informing, persuading, organizing, and providing enjoyment
- Listening and speaking: Listen with understanding and speak with clarity and purpose

*Problem Solving*

- Use problem-solving strategies both independently and collaboratively in academic areas and interpersonal relationships

*Mathematic and Scientific Reasoning*

- Demonstrate an understanding of the concepts of personal and environmental interdependence and an appreciation of cultural diversity in a global community
- Use a historical perspective to understand and apply fundamental American principles that lead to active, responsible citizenship

*Employability*

- Develop skills and attitudes necessary for successful employment and make career choices based on self-analysis and personal understanding

*Wellness*

- Apply knowledge and develop healthy habits of positive self-esteem and wellness for the purposes of making responsible lifestyle choices

*Technological Literacy*

- Use technology for lifelong learning and develop an understanding of technology's impact on the quality of life

*Fine Arts*

- Be active participants in exploring and developing individualized skill in creative expression and be able to respond to the creative work of others

*Lifelong Learning*

- Actively pursue and apply self-management, organizational skills, and learning as a lifelong process

*Personal/Social*

- Demonstrate self-discipline and apply knowledge and standards of conduct for the purpose of ethical decision making

SOURCE: Harrison School District 2, Colorado Springs, Colorado. Used by permission.

## APPENDIX B

## Key Quality Points of
## Performance-Based Curriculum

- Students are given quality models of performance based on real-world examples of excellence.

- Students practice toward, and teachers *teach* toward, those models. Criteria are clearly stated and set *in advance.*

- High standards are set and maintained and additional instructional support is provided for all students to meet standards.

- Students have the opportunity to reflect and practice self-evaluation.

- The engagement and motivation factors that have traditionally involved students in sports and the arts are applied to academic endeavors.

SOURCE: Harrison School District 2, Colorado Springs, Colorado. Used by permission.

# About the Authors

**Jeanne Guthrie** grew up in San Antonio, Texas, graduating from Thomas Jefferson High School in 1959. While in high school she met her husband, David. They have three children and are grandparents of two boys and a girl.

Having always wanted to teach, and encouraged by a grandmother who always shared the love of the children she taught, Jeanne obtained a B.S. degree in education from the University of Texas at Austin in 1964. Shortly thereafter, her husband's career moves led them first to Bridgeton, Missouri, where she attended the University of Missouri at St. Louis, receiving a master's degree in education in 1976, and then in 1988 to Colorado Springs, Colorado, where she met the coauthor of this book, Karen Perea.

She taught for 19 years in the Pattonville School District of Bridgeton, Missouri, and the past 7 years in the Harrison School District of Colorado Springs, Colorado. Today she is more excited about teaching than she was when she first began, with so much having changed for the better, and considers herself to be very blessed to have spent a lifetime doing the work of the heart—teaching.

**Karen M. Perea** was raised and educated in the community of Pueblo, Colorado in an area known as Bessemer Tech. While in high school she met her husband, Mark. They have one daughter.

Karen received a B.S degree in human development and child studies from Colorado State University in Fort Collins in 1981 and subsequently pursued a teaching certificate, which she received from Western State College in Gunnison, Colorado, in 1983.

Her teaching career has taken her to several places in Colorado—from the Front Range to the Western Slope and back again. In 1987, she and her husband were hired by the Harrison School District in Colorado Springs, where she has taught first grade for the past 8 years. Her devotion to children has led her to share her experiences and ideas to further enhance the teaching profession.

To our children and the children who touch our lives:
We hope your progression is continuous,
from chrysalis into free-thinking butterflies.

# CONNECTION

# 1

# Research

**Lifelong Learning**

Men and women can no longer be totally knowledgeable
of all that they will need to know
in our information and technological age.
The process of finding that information
is a part of learning.
Children must be exposed to
the research process as a means of
having a quality life.

# Outcomes of "Research" Connection

**LITERACY**

Research involves reading to find information, writing reports, and presenting the material orally.

**PERSONAL/SOCIAL**

Being able to interact with other students and being able to present information for the benefit of others are social skills that all students need.

**LIFELONG LEARNING**

In today's Information Age, the ability to find information is a skill that students will use their entire life.

**PROBLEM SOLVING**

Research involves deciding if material is appropriate to a topic, taking logical action to categorize and sequence, and judging completeness of a project.

**FINE ARTS**

The research rubrics enable students to identify a goal, the steps to accomplish the goal, and the selection of materials that will add to the oral presentation.

**MATHEMATIC/SCIENTIFIC REASONING**

Research on topics about the United States helps students to understand fundamental American principles that lead to responsible citizenship in a global community.

**EMPLOYABILITY**

Employers need employees who can read, write, present, and organize information to solve problems within the workplace.

**TECHNOLOGICAL LITERACY**

Using the computer to write and edit brings students into the world of technology. Using programs furthers their ability to find information.

Rubric 1.1

# "Research" Materials Needed

- **Primary Cycle**
  Large chart paper
  Books
  Magazines
  Videotapes, optional

- **Intermediate Cycle 1**
  Books—Insects
  Chart paper
  Markers

- **Intermediate Cycle 2**
  Books—American symbols
  Videotapes
  Materials from home
  Costumes, optional

- **Intermediate Cycle 3**
  Books—Heroes/heroines
  Tape recorder
  Tapes

- **Bonding Cycle 1**
  Books—Animals
  Chart paper
  Markers
  Magazines
  Note cards, optional

- **Bonding Cycle 2**
  Books—Plants
  Various brochures
  Seeds
  Soil
  Cups for planting
  Chart paper
  Construction paper
  Markers
  Note cards, optional

- **Bonding Cycle 3**
  Books—Countries
  Tag board
  Cardboard boxes
  Markers
  Note cards, optional

# "Research" Primary Cycle
## *Student Task*

## TASK

All of us enjoy different things. It's what makes getting to know each other fun and interesting. Your favorite activity may be rollerblading or bike riding or snowboarding. Whatever it may be there is probably something written about it to tell of its history, detail the way it's done, who (if anyone) invented it, and how you might go about learning how to participate in it.

Think of one thing you enjoy doing. Then gather up as much information as possible on your topic. Go to the library and find books, magazines, pictures, and whatever else you can think of as support. Once you find all of the materials you can on your topic, think of an interesting way that you can tell us about it. You may give an actual demonstration, show a videotape of you performing your favorite activity, or make a display of pictures and actual items needed for your activity. You will be scored on your knowledge of the topic and on your creativity in presenting the information to us.

## CRITERIA

Knowledge of topic

Ability to share information

Oral presentation

# "Research" Primary Cycle
## *Teaching Suggestions*

This activity prepares primary students for the unit on research that they will do with their big buddies. Primary students are very curious by nature, which is an asset when it comes to their research project. Young children love to question their surroundings and environment; therefore, this project helps them focus their questions. This project, done with the whole group, teaches the students how to answer any and all of the questions they may have about a particular topic.

To introduce researching skills, pick a topic that may be of interest to the majority of your students. Past topics have been spiders, turtles, ants, and ladybugs. Once the topic has been chosen, take the class to the library to select the materials needed to conduct the research. Introduce them to the card catalog, explaining how to find books on the chosen topic, and where in the library to locate them. When the materials have been chosen, check them out and return to the classroom to begin the project.

Once the materials have been displayed and the students know what they will be studying, ask them what they know about the topic and record their answers on the overhead or large chart paper. Next, encourage them to tell what they want to know about the topic and again record their responses for the class to see. Explain to your students that from the chart of what they want to know will come their research questions. To make this point clear, write out the questions (the ones they will be answering) on large chart paper as a reminder of what information they will need to be listening for.

Read aloud as many of the selected books as possible during various times of the day. After some information has been shared, ask if any of the questions written on the chart paper can be answered. Record the answers to any the students heard from the materials being shared. Continue sharing information until all the questions have been answered. Then show the students how to web the new information with what they already knew. From this web will come their written report. With your guidance, and with you as the recorder, students take the information from the web and begin writing the paragraphs of the report.

Because this process takes several days to a week and because it is a very challenging activity for primary students, there is no additional task for first graders. However, if you teach second or third grade, you may want to give an individual project a try (see the task included). The first-grade students are assessed on their listening skills, participation skills, and knowledge gained from the research project. To assess the knowledge gained on the topic, play 20 Questions ("I'm thinking of a . . . ") or other games that check comprehension in a very stress-free way. Second- and third-grade students can also be assessed this way, or you may choose to assess them on the individual task if you opted to use it.

## Analysis and Reflection: "Research" Primary Cycle—Group Project

| STANDARDS: The levels at which students perform the task | | | | |
|---|---|---|---|---|
| **In Progress** | **Basic** | **Proficient** | **Advanced** | **Comments** |
| During the presentation, the student appears distracted and/or distracts others by talking to self or others and turning away from the speaker. | During the entire presentation, the student demonstrates listening by staying quiet with hands still and turning toward the speaker and regularly maintaining eye contact. | During the entire presentation, the student demonstrates listening by staying quiet with hands and body still and turning toward the speaker and maintaining consistent eye contact. | There are highly observable, appropriate nonverbal responses. | |
| There is little or no evidence of nonverbal responses (smiles, nods, etc.). | There are some appropriate nonverbal responses. | | | |
| During the majority of the presentation, the student demonstrates listening by staying quiet with hands still and turning toward the speaker. | | | | |
| There is limited evidence of nonverbal responses. | | | | |

**Rubric 1.2**
NOTE: Analysis and Reflection is to be used if task is not assigned.

Analysis and Reflection: "Research" Primary Cycle—Favorite Activity

**STANDARDS: The levels at which students perform the task**

| In Progress | Basic | Proficient | Advanced | Comments |
|---|---|---|---|---|
| Student can locate very little information on topic, much of which is inappropriate. | Student can locate some information on topic, some of which is appropriate. | Student can locate information on topic, most of which is appropriate. | Student can locate much information on topic, all of which is appropriate. | |
| Student displays little knowledge of topic. Student cannot answer questions. Oral presentation lacks creativity. | Student displays some knowledge of topic, either background or new. | Student displays knowledge of topic, both background and new. | Student displays extensive knowledge of topic. | |
| | Student can answer some questions. | Student can answer questions but cannot elaborate. | Student can answer any question and add more details. | |
| There is no eye contact. | Oral presentation shows some creativity. | Oral presentation is clear/concise, with creativity evident. | Oral presentation is creative in all aspects. | |
| Voice is not clear. | There is limited eye contact. | Student maintains eye contact most of the time. | Eye contact is maintained for the entire presentation. | |
| There is no visual display. | Voice is somewhat clear. | Voice is clear. | Voice is clear and expressive. | |
| | Visual display is some-what appealing. | Visual display is neat and appealing. | Visual display shows effort and creativity. | |

**Rubric 1.3**

# "Research" Intermediate Cycle 1
## *Student Task*

## TASK

Even in our Information Age it is impossible to know everything about every subject, but it is possible to have access to that information. Using books, articles, encyclopedias, magazines, computer programs, and other resources, we can discover whatever we need to know about any subject. This process of tracking down information is called "research."

When we research, we read all of the writings of researchers to see what they have discovered about the subject we are interested in. We then put the newly acquired information into our own words for later use. There are many ways to make the readings our own. We can web, outline, use note cards, or write sentences that paraphrase what we have read.

Your task is to begin to learn how to research. First, select any insect that is of interest to you. Go to the library and begin to read from all the insect resources you can find. As you find information that you think others might find interesting, jot it down in brief notes. You will want to consider what the insect eats, where it lives, its life cycle, its means of reproduction, and its value to the ecosystem in which it lives.

After your reading and note taking has been completed, write 20 sentences, using your own words, to tell about the insect. Make your sentences detailed, informative, and interesting. Then study your sentences and organize them by category of information they provide. For instance, all of the sentences that describe your insect might go under a category called "Characteristics." Those that tell about the life cycle might go under a heading called "Life Cycle." Finally, put your sentences and their categories onto chart paper. Illustrate the chart with drawings or pictures that will explain the information. Be prepared to share your information with the class. The information on the charts will be made available for other classes.

## CRITERIA

Knowledge of insect

Ability to paraphrase

Ability to categorize

Oral presentation

Visual chart

# "Research" Intermediate Cycle 1
*Teaching Suggestions*

This activity is an extension of categorizing and an introduction to taking notes and researching. Begin by reading a book to the students that is fairly simple but gives the basic characteristics of insects. As you read, point out the different categories that could be used for paragraphs about insects: characteristics, life cycle, food, usefulness, habitat, enemies, and so on. You might even want to put these into outline form so that students will know what information they should look for in their reading. It will also help them categorize their sentences later. (You can use the outline provided or create your own using the blank outline supplied.) After you outline, ask students to paraphrase parts of the outline using as many different sentences as they can. Compare these for accuracy, variety, detail, and originality. Point out the categories and show how the various sentences could be grouped together because they have in common one topic about insects.

Next, show the students informational charts that you use in the classroom. Emphasize that these charts not only provide information but also show illustrations that make the information more understandable. Now take the sentences that you have written together and decide how they could best be organized on a large poster board. Draw or cut out pictures to illustrate the students' sentences.

Finally, hand out the rubric and allow time for the students to study the task. Either bring materials to the room or take students to the library to begin their own research. It is important that they have plenty of time to read and take notes. Too often, students want to read only one source of information. They should be encouraged to find as many resources as they can, read from all of them, and take brief notes to remind them of the information acquired. The outline form can be used to ensure that students cover all of the information about the insect they have chosen. They will then need several periods to organize their information into sentences. During this time, they should be encouraged to self- and peer edit for mistakes in spelling, punctuation, and grammar. Remind them that they will be writing for an audience and their information should be in correct form. Have the students categorize their sentences with major headings and organize them onto large poster boards. When all the writing has been transferred to the chart, encourage the students to illustrate or cut out pictures to further illustrate the information they have acquired. The result will be charts that could go into the library for others to use. Stress accuracy, neatness, and eye appeal.

# Analysis and Reflection: "Research" Intermediate Cycle—Activity 1: Insect Research

## STANDARDS: The levels at which students perform the task

| In Progress | Basic | Proficient | Advanced | Comments |
|---|---|---|---|---|
| Student knows few or no characteristics of insects. | Student knows some of the characteristics of insects. | Student knows most of the characteristics of insects. | Student knows all the characteristics of insects. | |
| Student is only able to copy sentences. | Student is able to paraphrase information. | Student is able to paraphrase information into sentences. | Student is able to paraphrase information into descriptive, original sentences. | |
| Student is unable to categorize sentences and/or give headings. | Student is able to categorize sentences into at least two groups. | Student is able to categorize sentences into a few groups with headings. | Student is able to categorize sentences into groups and provide interesting and informative headings. | |
| Chart is incomplete or missing. | Chart is acceptable. | Chart is attractive. | Chart is visually very appealing. | |
| There are few or no pictures or drawings to add to sentence information. | Pictures and drawings are on the chart and generally add to the sentence information. | Pictures and drawings add to the sentence information. | Pictures or drawings show effort and add to the sentence information. | |
| Information is read word-for-word, with little evidence of preparation. | The information is read but in an interesting way. | Information is mostly presented, although some parts might be read. | The information is presented in an interesting way rather than read. | |
| There is little or no eye contact. | Eye contact is made periodically. | Eye contact is made but may not be maintained. | Student maintains eye contact. | |
| Voice lacks expression and is difficult to hear. | Speaker can be heard by the audience. | Speaker can be heard by the audience. | Speaker uses an expressive voice that can be heard clearly by the audience. | |
| Errors in spelling, punctuation, and grammar interfere with the meaning. | There are some errors in spelling, punctuation, and grammar, but they do not distract from meaning. | Sentences have few errors in spelling, punctuation, and grammar. | There is evidence of editing, with minimal or no errors in spelling, punctuation, or grammar. | |

**Rubric 1.4**

# "Research" Intermediate Cycle 1
## *Outline Example*

- **Topic:** *Insects*

1. Question to be answered: *What do I generally know and feel about butterflies?*

   **Outlined information**
   I. *Butterflies*
      A.
      B.
      C.
      D.

2. Question to be answered: *What are the parts of the butterfly?*

   **Outlined information**
   II. *Parts of the butterfly*
      A.
      B.
      C.
      D.

3. Question to be answered: *Where does a butterfly live naturally?*

   **Outlined information**
   III. *Natural environment*
      A.
      B.
      C.
      D.

4. Question to be answered: *How and why are butterflies important?*

   **Outlined information**
   IV. *Importance*
       A.

       B.

       C.

       D.

5. Question to be answered: *What are four different kinds of butterflies? How are they different from one another?*

   **Outlined information**
   V. *Kinds*
       A.

       B.

       C.

       D.

6. Question to be answered: *How can I summarize my information about butterflies?*

   **Outlined information**
   VI. *Concluding paragraph—summary*
       A.

       B.

       C.

       D.

**Figure 1.1**

# "Research" Intermediate Cycle 1
*Outline*

- **Topic:**

1. Question to be answered:


   **Outlined information**
   I.
   - A.
   - B.
   - C.
   - D.

2. Question to be answered:


   **Outlined information**
   II.
   - A.
   - B.
   - C.
   - D.

3. Question to be answered:


   **Outlined information**
   III.
   - A.
   - B.
   - C.
   - D.

4. Question to be answered:

**Outlined information**
IV.
    A.

    B.

    C.

    D.

5. Question to be answered:

**Outlined information**
V.
    A.

    B.

    C.

    D.

6. Question to be answered:

**Outlined information**
VI.
    A.

    B.

    C.

    D.

**Figure 1.2**

# "Research" Intermediate Cycle 2
## *Student Task*

## TASK

A symbol is something that stands for some object or idea. One of the most familiar symbols is a country's flag. There are, however, other symbols that people associate with a country.

Your task is to research symbols of the United States. Some are very obvious, but others not so obvious are equally important to visitors who come to America for the first time. Try to discover those symbols that others can't wait to see but you might take for granted. After you have collected your information, be prepared to share it in a video presentation. You will want to make a copy of your symbol, whether it is using popsicle sticks to construct the White House or baking an apple pie and explaining its significance to Americans. Finally, acting as someone from the past will make your presentation even more exciting. You will be able to wear a period costume and use a different voice. Try to find something unique to research to make your prototype and oral presentation creative.

## CRITERIA

Selection of symbol

Model of symbol

Oral presentation

# "Research" Intermediate Cycle 2
## *Teaching Suggestions*

This second activity in research is one that is always very popular with intermediate students because it gives them the opportunity to create a videotape. Being able to see the results of their reading and note taking is quite exciting. You will find that students are quite creative once they get over being nervous about seeing themselves on television. Hopefully, this will not be totally new for everyone. If this experience is totally new to some, it is helpful to hold practice sessions so that students can critique themselves and each other before making the final tape. (If no video cameras are available, this activity can be an oral presentation.)

Before handing out the rubric, either teach or review the use of the 5 Ws: who, what, when, where, and why. It is always important to model this process with students before they actually begin to read and write on their own. You might begin by reading a fairly simple book on the American flag. As you read, point out the following:

- WHO designed and made the first American flag?
- WHAT was the meaning of the stars and stripes?
- WHEN was the first flag designed and made?
- WHERE was the flag first displayed?
- WHY was the first flag designed and made?

Of course, don't stop here. Encourage students to read further and to create a series of questions that they want answered about the flag—for instance, "Has the flag changed since it was first designed? Why has it changed?" The questions are endless, and one leads to another.

Once the students have their information, they need to decide together how they want to display it to an audience. Do they want to make a copy or use unbleached muslin and crayons to make several examples, or do they want to put their information in chart form? You might want to have one class period devoted to making one of the various American flags from history. Students love copying the design onto material and coloring it with crayons. Then all you need to do is place waxed paper over the design and iron in the color and hang the flags around the room.

Another question to consider is whether or not students would consider dressing like a colonial soldier or other colonist to make the presentation about the flag. Developing other personae with costumes and accents make the presentations interesting for everyone watching the video.

After you have modeled the process, hand out the rubric and encourage students to search for unusual symbols that represent the United States. Most will know of the Liberty Bell and the White House, but have they thought about a horseshoe as a symbol of good luck or the horn of plenty to celebrate Thanksgiving? Ask students to read and be original with not only their symbol but the way they display that information.

When students have completed their research, developed models or pictures, and become a persona to present the information about the symbol, allow time for them to practice in small groups before making the videotape. Finally, tape their performances and make the tape available for students to take home for family viewing. You might also call local military facilities and make the tape available for their use as a motivational message about the United States.

# Analysis and Reflection: "Research" Intermediate Cycle—Activity 2: America Research

## STANDARDS: The levels at which students perform the task

| In Progress | Basic | Proficient | Advanced | Comments |
|---|---|---|---|---|
| Student recognizes and selects the flag as an American symbol to research even though it was used to model.<br><br>The model is incomplete and/or incorrect and shows little or no effort.<br><br>Information presented is difficult to follow and lacks organization.<br><br>No costume is used for the presentation.<br><br>Information is read word-for-word, with little evidence of preparation.<br><br>There is little or no eye contact.<br><br>Voice lacks expression and is difficult to hear.<br><br>Little or no evidence of the 5Ws (who, what, when, where, why) is presented. | Student recognizes the most familiar symbols of America and selects one of these to research.<br><br>Model has some details and is mostly complete.<br><br>Some effort is evident.<br><br>Information presented is accurate, and the order of the presentation does not take away from its meaning.<br><br>There is minimal use of costumes in the presentation.<br><br>Information is read but in an interesting way.<br><br>Eye contact is made periodically.<br><br>Speaker can be heard by the audience.<br><br>Some evidence of answering the 5Ws is presented. | Student recognizes symbols of America and shows originality in the selection of a symbol to research.<br><br>The model is detailed, complete, and correct and shows effort.<br><br>Information is mostly clear and sequential. Costumes add to the presentation.<br><br>Information is mostly presented rather than read.<br><br>Eye contact is made but may not be maintained.<br><br>Speaker uses a voice that can be heard by the audience.<br><br>Information presented covers the 5Ws and covers the topic. | Student is able to recognize symbols of America and selects an unusual symbol to research.<br><br>The model is well detailed, complete, correct, and shows great effort.<br><br>Information is presented in a clear, logical, and sequential order.<br><br>Costumes are used effectively in the presentation.<br><br>Information is presented in an interesting way rather than read.<br><br>Student maintains eye contact.<br><br>Speaker uses an expressive voice that can be heard clearly by the audience.<br><br>Information presented includes the 5Ws and completely covers the topic. | |

Rubric 1.5

18

# "Research" Intermediate Cycle 3
## *Student Task*

## TASK

The United States has many heroes from its past and in the present. Some are very famous, but others have made contributions that aren't as well known. All of these people are responsible for making our country free and powerful.

For your final research project, you are to find and interview someone who has made a contribution to America. If possible, bring this person to school.

Remember during your search that there are local heroes: the policeman who saved a dog from drowning, the fireman who saves a child, or even the next-door neighbor who helped you one rainy day when you were locked out of the house. All of these people make our lives safer and happier.

Once you have found your "hero," find out all that you can about this person and what contributions he or she made to our nation. Be prepared to share your information with your classmates. If your hero is able to come to class, you will be responsible for introducing your guest to your classmates. You will also need to write up your information as a biography that you will present to your hero. A tape recording can be made if your guest is unable to come in person.

## CRITERIA

Completion of project

Ability to interview

Written biography

# "Research" Intermediate Cycle 3
## *Teaching Suggestions*

This is an easy activity to begin with because students love to talk about events that have happened in their lives. Ask them to tell about a time they did something important or daring, such as saving a little sister or brother from running out into the street or helping a neighbor who was ill and unable to do necessary chores. Conversation should be lively.

When students have had the opportunity to talk about themselves, extend the conversation to people they have heard about who are heroes or heroines. You might even bring in a newspaper article about such a person as an example. Hand out the rubric and explain that students are to find a real hero or heroine from their family, friends, or neighborhood who has helped make life better for someone else.

Explain to students that they will be responsible for asking a set of questions about the heroic event to introduce the guest to the class. (They can use the set of questions that follow or create a list with the class as a whole. A third option is to create their own list after a discussion of what is important.) They will then need to interview the person they have selected and create a biography of that person's life, with special emphasis on the event that made the individual a hero or heroine.

A final but exciting part of the project is to bring the hero into the classroom to be introduced to the rest of the class. (You will need to coordinate these visits according to class schedules and time available.) As guests arrive, students should introduce their hero or heroine and explain some of that individual's background and the heroic event itself. If pictures or news articles are available, be sure to include these with the presentation. Schedule enough time for a question and answer period after the presentation. At this time, the student who found the hero can present the guest with the written biography. If possible, videotape all of the guests' interviews for viewing at the end of the year.

Analysis and Reflection: "Research" Intermediate Cycle—Activity 3: Hero Research

| STANDARDS: The levels at which students perform the task | | | | |
|---|---|---|---|---|
| **In Progress** | **Basic** | **Proficient** | **Advanced** | **Comments** |
| Purpose of the task is not achieved in the interview and/or biography. | Purpose of the project is achieved in the interview and biography. | Purpose of the project is evident in the interview and biography. | Purpose of the project is totally achieved in the interview and biography. | |
| Interview questions are too incomplete to bring out the basic information. | Interview questions bring out the basic information. | Interview questions bring out the most important information. | Interview questions are well detailed to provide the most important information. | |
| There is little evidence of preparation in the interview. | There is some evidence of preparation in the interview. | There is evidence of preparation and interest in the interview. | Student shows evidence of preparation, organization, and enthusiasm in the interview. | |
| Delivery by the speaker is awkward. | The speaker can be heard by the audience some of the time. | Speaker can be heard by the audience. | Speaker uses a voice that can be heard by the entire audience. | |
| Student asks few or no questions of the person being interviewed. | Student asks prepared questions of the person being interviewed. | Student is aware of the responses of the person being interviewed and can ask some questions based on those responses. | Student asks questions based on the responses of the person interviewed. | |
| Biography is incomplete and includes little or no information. | Biography includes the information obtained by the student. | Biography is constructed in an original way. | Biography is put together in an original and creative way. | |
| Errors in spelling, punctuation, and grammar consistently interfere with the meaning. | Some errors in spelling, punctuation, and grammar occasionally interfere with the meaning. | Errors in spelling, punctuation, and grammar do not interfere with the meaning. | There are minimal or no errors in spelling, punctuation, and grammar. | |

**Rubric 1.6**

21

# "Research" Biography Interview Guide

1. Why is this person a hero or heroine?

2. How has this person made a difference to someone's life?

3. What are some of the character traits that make this person a hero or heroine?

4. What is the family background of this person?

5. Why did you choose this person?

6. What do you like or admire about this person?

7. What lessons did you learn from this person?

8. Do you think that you could have done the heroic action that this person did?

# "Research" Bonding Cycle
## *Overview*

Before you say "*Impossible!*", know that even first graders can do research in the library and do it artfully. By the time this activity is presented to the little buddies, the big buddies have already performed tasks that use the library in a research project. When they see the requirements on the bonding activity, they see that the visual chart, the reading and writing, and the oral presentations follow a pattern similar to ones that they have already completed. They also know their little buddies and their abilities.

Present the idea of asking four questions that the little buddy would like to have answered about an animal, a plant, or a country. Then turn the buddy pairs loose in the library. Remind the big buddies that they are the facilitators. They should read the materials, showing their little buddies how to find the answers to the questions.

When the pairs have completed their reading and note taking, they make their visual presentations. Then the buddies should decide how they will present their information in the oral presentation. Little buddies should know what they want to say and have a part in the oral performance. Again, videotaping and critiquing their run-throughs help the buddy pairs evaluate their own presentation and decide how they could better meet the standards set forth in the rubric. When the big day arrives, videotape them, assess their performances, and confer with the buddy pairs.

# "Research" Bonding Cycle 1
## *Student Task*

## TASK

You and your buddy are going to help make a poster display of animals for the library. The two of you will be responsible for selecting an unusual animal that you would like to know more about. After you have chosen an animal, you need to decide on at least four questions that you would like to have answered about the animal. With your buddy you need to read together, take notes on note cards, and prepare a written answer to the questions that you have researched. You are to keep a list of the books that you and your buddy use. This is called a bibliography and should include the title of the book, the author, and pages read. Use the form given to you by the teacher.

You and your buddy then need to prepare a chart to present to an audience. You might want to draw a picture of the animal for the middle of the chart and place the questions and answers elsewhere on the chart. You can add other pictures or drawings that you feel would help explain your new information.

When the chart is completed, practice what you will say to the audience to explain your animal. You need to look at the audience and speak in a loud, clear voice so everyone can hear you.

## CRITERIA

Research skills

Visual presentation (chart)

Knowledge of animal

Oral presentation

Cooperation

# "Research" Bonding Cycle 1
## *Teaching Suggestions*

To begin this activity, have the buddy pairs talk about their pets. Everyone will want to add to the conversation—you will probably have a hard time getting them to stop. Little buddies quickly follow their big buddies in wanting to share their own experiences. They seem to become empowered by listening to the older students.

After the pet discussion, ask the students if there are any other animals they would like to learn more about. You might even want to list these as the students mention them. Explain that they are going to get the opportunity to read about an animal that is new to them, and the more unusual the animal, the more interesting their research will be.

Hand out the list of questions and discuss them briefly. Explain that the big buddies will help the little buddies decide on at least four questions that they would like to have answered about the animal they are going to study. When buddy pairs have selected their questions, the next step is going to the library to read for the answers. Older buddies, who already know how to take notes, should encourage their little buddies to also keep notes as they read. Note cards can be purchased or made by cutting out lined notebook paper.

When notes have been taken and the buddy pairs have the information they need, give them a large poster board on which they can put their information in chart form, which they will share orally with the rest of the class. They might draw a picture of the animal in the center of the chart paper and then place the questions and the answers to the questions around the picture. Other illustrations will add to the information presented.

Students should practice their oral presentations when the charts are completed. The little buddy could read the question and the big buddy discuss the answer or vice versa. We do not advise letting the big buddy share all of the information on the chart because the little buddy will be left out and discipline problems might arise. Stress the importance of maintaining eye contact and speaking in a loud enough voice to be heard by the audience. When students have had ample time to practice, videotape the presentations. It's very exciting to invite parents to these sessions. They are in awe when they realize that a first grader has done a research report! Not only that, the parents of your more talented students will not say their children are not being challenged!

# Analysis and Reflection: "Research" Bonding Cycle—Activity 1: Animal Research

## STANDARDS: The levels at which students perform the task

| In Progress | Basic | Proficient | Advanced | Comments |
|---|---|---|---|---|
| No references are cited. Few or no notes are kept. Chart is incomplete or missing. Little information about the animal is presented. One or no question is answered about the animal. Errors in spelling, punctuation, and grammar significantly interfere with the meaning. Buddies read the information awkwardly, with little evidence of preparation. Little or no eye contact is made. Voices are difficult to understand. Both buddies are unfocused on the task. | Some books, authors, and pages read are listed. At least two references are cited. Notes are kept on paper rather than note cards. Chart is entirely made by the older buddy. Most knowledge of the animal is commonly known. At least two questions are answered. Errors in spelling, punctuation, and grammar occasionally interfere with the meaning. Buddies read information but in an interesting way. Eye contact is made periodically. Voices are heard the majority of the time. Both buddies are able to work on the task but may talk some of the time. | Record of books, authors, and pages read is kept but may be incomplete. Several references are cited. Note cards are used but primarily by the older buddy. Chart is primarily done by the older buddy. Some new knowledge of the animal is presented. At least three questions are answered. Errors in spelling, punctuation, and grammar do not interfere with the meaning. Both buddies tell the majority of their information rather than read it. Eye contact is made but not maintained. Voices are heard and generally understood. Both buddies are focused on the task the majority of the time. | Complete record of books, authors, and pages read is kept. Numerous references are cited. Note cards are used by both buddies. Both buddies write on the chart. There is evidence of new information on the animal. At least four questions are answered. There are minimal or no errors in spelling, punctuation, and grammar. Both buddies tell about their animal in an engaging way, without reading from notes. Eye contact is maintained. Voices can be heard easily. Both buddies are totally engaged in the task. | |

Rubric 1.7

# "Research" Bonding Cycle 1
## *Questions on Animals*

The following questions might be helpful in getting started with your research. You *do not* have to answer all of them. You and your buddy may select those that are of interest to you and decide how to present your knowledge of the answers in words and with illustrations.

What does your animal look like?

What are the parts of your animal?

What does your animal eat?

Where does your animal find its food?

Where does your animal live naturally?

What are the habits of your animal?

What does your animal do during the day?

What does your animal do during the night?

Are there different kinds of your animal?

Can your animal be found in the zoo?

Is your animal close to extinction?

Is your animal ever a pet? How would you care for it if it is?

What is the skeletal build of your animal?

How does your animal reproduce?

What are the general facts about your animal: size, weight, number of offspring, length of life, and scientific classification?

How could you track your animal?

How would you describe the geographical region in which your animal is found?

Does your animal have an interesting history?

If there is any question you and your buddy have that is not included above, please check with your teacher.

# "Research" Bonding Cycle 1
## *Bibliography*

Name

Buddy's Name

| Title of Book | Author(s) | Pages Read |
|---|---|---|
| 1. | | |
| 2. | | |
| 3. | | |
| 4. | | |
| 5. | | |
| 6. | | |
| 7. | | |
| 8. | | |
| 9. | | |
| 10. | | |

**Figure 1.3**

# "Research" Bonding Cycle 1

*Suggested Books*

| | |
|---|---|
| *A Kid's Guide to How to Save the Animals* | Billy Goodman |
| *Kids Can Save the Animals!* | Ingrid Newkirk |
| *For Kids Who Love Animals* | Linda Koebner |
| *Science for Kids: 39 Biology Experiences* | Robert Wood |
| *Save the Earth* | Betty Miles |
| *The Kids' World Almanac of Animals and Pets* | Deborah Felder |
| *The City Kids' Field Guide* | Ethan Heberman |
| *The Kids' Question and Answer Book:*<br>  *A Dog for the Kids* | Mordecai Siegal |
| *The Animal Kids* | Lorinda Cauley |
| *Zoo Keeper* | Software; Davidson, $54.95 |
| *Kid's Zoo* | Software; Davidson, $42.95 |

# "Research" Bonding Cycle 2
## *Student Task*

### TASK

You and your buddy have been commissioned by a company that publishes information about plants. The company wants to be able to present individual brochures to anyone inquiring about plant life. The two of you will be responsible for selecting questions you want answered, reading together, taking notes on index cards, and writing the final, edited brochure that will be available to the public. You may choose any form of plant that the two of you are interested in knowing more about. Part of the challenge of your task is to include your buddy in the steps you will use. You can encourage your buddy to do some of the actual writing, draw illustrations, and decide on the questions you want to research. If you are able, you can plant seeds or bring in examples of your plants to present to the company along with your pamphlet. Your work must be totally correct for publication, but remember that your buddy is in a primary grade and his or her work will not be up to the standard that you require for yourself. It is always important to be positive when working with your buddy.

You are to keep a list of the books that you and your buddy use. This is called a bibliography and should include the title of the book, the author, and pages read. Use the form given to you by the teacher. You may use the computers when they are available, but you must write your brochure by hand when they are not.

### CRITERIA

Research skills

Visual display

Oral presentation

Cooperation

# "Research" Bonding Cycle 2
## *Teaching Suggestions*

Begin this activity just as you began the one on animal research, by encouraging students to talk about the kinds of plants they know. After having participated in the first research, students are very excited to begin another project with their buddies. Write their responses on the board. Then begin to group the different plants into categories: trees, flowers, weeds, cacti, shrubs, and so on. Categorizing is a higher-level thinking skill and one that all of the students will need to use across the curriculum. Again, students are to select a category and a plant within that category. Explain that this time they are going to read, take notes, and make a brochure besides giving an oral presentation. They will have the added responsibility to bring in an example of their plant or to grow seeds of their plant. Having plants growing in the classroom adds excitement as children can observe them daily, noting the changes as the plants grow.

You will need to bring in brochures as examples. These can be obtained from any local hotel. Point out that the brochures have pictures along with written explanations. Remind the students that they are going to make their brochure about the plant they have chosen, adding the information found from reading about that plant. They will already have an idea about placing information since they will have completed the chart in the first research activity.

Folding a large piece of construction paper into thirds is an easy way to make a brochure. We recommend that students write on lined paper, cut it out, and place it on the brochure as they finish. This process results in a neater project, and the students will not feel the need to draw lines before they write.

When the brochures are completed, give the students time to practice their oral presentations before they actually present their projects. Remind them that if they have grown a plant or have brought in examples of their plant they will be expected to share this information during their oral presentation.

# Analysis and Reflection: "Research" Bonding Cycle—Activity 2: Plant Research

| STANDARDS: The levels at which students perform the task | | | | |
|---|---|---|---|---|
| In Progress | Basic | Proficient | Advanced | Comments |
| No references are cited. Few or no notes are kept. Brochure is incomplete or missing. Little information about plants is given in the brochure. One or no question is answered about the plant. Errors in spelling, punctuation, and grammar significantly interfere with the meaning. Buddies read the information on the brochure awkwardly, with little evidence of preparation. Little or no eye contact is made. Voices are difficult to understand. Both buddies are unfocused on making the visual display. | Some books, authors, and pages read are listed. At least two references are cited. Notes are kept on paper rather than note cards. Brochure is entirely made by the older buddy. One or two illustrations are added to the visual display. At least two questions are answered. Errors in spelling, punctuation, and grammar occasionally interfere with the meaning. Buddies read their brochure but in an interesting way. Eye contact is made periodically. Voices are heard the majority of the time. Both buddies work on the brochure but may talk some of the time. Buddies only complete the brochure without extra plans. | Record of books, authors, and pages read is kept but may be incomplete. Several references are cited. Note cards are used but primarily by the older buddy. Brochure is primarily done by the older buddy. Some illustrations are added to the brochure. At least three questions are answered. Errors in spelling, punctuation, and grammar do not interfere with the meaning. Both buddies tell about the majority of the brochure and only read portions. Eye contact is made but not maintained. Voices are heard and generally understood. Both buddies are focused on the task/brochure. Buddies do something extra to enhance their presentation. | Complete record of books, authors, and pages read is kept. Numerous references are cited. Note cards are used by both buddies. Both buddies contribute to the brochure. Brochure is visually very appealing. Illustrations add to the information presented. At least four questions are answered. There are minimal or no errors in spelling, punctuation, and grammar. Both buddies can explain their brochure without reading the information. Eye contact is maintained. Voices can be heard easily. Both buddies are totally engaged in the task. Buddies grow seeds and bring examples of plants to further enhance their presentation. | |

Rubric 1.8

32

# "Research" Questions on Plants

The following questions might be helpful in getting started with your research. You *do not* have to answer all of them. You and your buddy may select those that are of interest to you and decide how you will use the information in your brochure. Remember that you will need to include illustrations and experiment results, if you decide to do one.

What kind of plant (grass, tree, shrub, etc.) are you researching?

What is the appearance and structure of your plant?

What are the parts of your plant?

How does your plant make and use food?

How does your plant reproduce?

Where are your plants found?

How does your plant depend on the soil?

How does your plant depend on light?

How does your plant depend on water?

How is your plant important?

Is your plant beneficial to humans? In what ways?

How is your plant in danger in our world?

What are the products made from your plant?

What are the enemies of your plant?

What are the diseases of your plant?

What is the classification of your plant?

How can your plant be harmful to humans?

How is your plant grown?

What is the climate of the area where your plant is found naturally?

What are the different kinds of your plant?

# "Research" Bonding Cycle 2
## *Suggested Books*

| | |
|---|---|
| *Let's Get Growing* | Joel Rapp |
| *Growing Indoor Plants* | Jane Courtier |
| *The Plant and Grow Project Book* | Ulla Dietl |
| *Flowers, Trees and Other Plants* | John Stidworthy |
| *Science for Kids* | Robert Wood |
| *Get Growing! Exciting Indoor Plant Projects* | Lois Walker |
| *Growing Plants* | Barbara Taylor |
| *Learn About Plants* | Software; Leaningways, Inc., $79.00 |

# "Research" Bonding Cycle 3
## *Student Task*

## TASK

You and your buddy have been selected to create a display for International Day at school. You are to be responsible for selecting questions, taking notes on index cards, and creating a display about the country you have chosen. Part of the challenge of your task is to include your buddy in creating the display. After you have completed your research and note taking, you will decide how you wish to present your new knowledge. You can create a chart, a booklet, a tape, or a video. You will be expected to share your information with both classes. Your work must be totally correct for the presentation, but remember that your buddy is in a primary grade and his or her work will not be up to the standard that you require for yourself. It is always important to be positive when working with your buddy.

Try to make your display stand alone, with titles, pictures, drawings, graphs, or stories, but be prepared to answer questions and discuss the country you have chosen. You may bring in props such as costumes, dolls, relics, or food that come from the country you are researching.

You are to keep a list of the books that you and your buddy use. Put the book titles, authors, and pages read on the bibliography form provided by the teacher.

## CRITERIA

Research skills

Visual display

Oral presentation

Cooperation

# "Research" Bonding Cycle 3
## *Teaching Suggestions*

By the time you begin this third buddy research, the students will feel very comfortable with reading for information. As you introduce the idea of reading about countries, it is a good idea to have a map or globe nearby so that students can actually see the areas referred to. Even older students sometimes confuse countries with continents or states with countries. Again, encourage students to talk about different countries and different ways of life in those countries. If you have students from other countries, this is an excellent way to begin this activity. As the different nations are suggested, write them on the board. Buddy pairs then select one that they would like to learn more about. If students seem to be having difficulty thinking of countries, you might want to point some out and add these to your board list.

Explain that buddies will have a set of questions to help them begin. Again, they should select a minimum of four to answer, but this time they will be making a display for everyone to see. A display can be presented in a cardboard box or on a poster board that has been bent in the middle. Either way, the students are to decorate their board with pictures, drawings, their questions, and the answers to those questions. In our particular school, we celebrate "International Day," and students visit other rooms to see how other classes celebrate the cultures of others. If this is not possible for your entire school, invite classes in to see the displays. Students can stand by their displays and explain what they have discovered about their country. Do practice, however.

This activity can be accomplished in daily meetings or an entire day can be devoted to making the displays. You will know the ability of your students to stay focused for a longer period of time.

Finally, you might plan on a family evening, inviting the parents to walk around the room to hear the different information presented in the displays.

# Analysis and Reflection: "Research" Bonding Cycle—Activity 3: Country Research

## STANDARDS: The levels at which students perform the task

| In Progress | Basic | Proficient | Advanced | Comments |
|---|---|---|---|---|
| No references are cited. Few or no notes are kept. Visual display is incomplete or missing. One or no question is answered about the country. Errors in spelling, punctuation, and grammar significantly interfere with the meaning. Buddies read the information from the visual display awkwardly, with little evidence of preparation. Little or no eye contact is made. Voices are difficult to understand. Both buddies are unfocused on making the visual display. | Some books, authors, and pages read are listed. At least two references are cited. Notes are kept on paper rather than note cards. Visual display is entirely made by the older buddy. A few pictures or drawings add to the visual display. At least two questions are answered. Errors in spelling, punctuation, and grammar occasionally interfere with the meaning. Buddies read information from the visual display but in an interesting way. Eye contact is made periodically. Voices are heard the majority of the time. Both buddies complete the visual display but may talk some of the time. | Record of books, authors, and pages read is kept but may be incomplete. Several references are cited. Note cards are used but primarily by the older buddy. Visual display is primarily done by the older buddy. Some pictures, drawings, or demonstrations add to the visual display. At least three questions are answered. Errors in spelling, punctuation, and grammar do not interfere with the meaning. Both buddies can tell about their country but may read some parts of the visual display. Eye contact is made but not maintained. Voices are heard and generally understood. Both buddies are focused on making the visual display. | Complete record of books, authors, and pages read is kept. Numerous references are cited. Note cards are used by both buddies. Both buddies contribute to the visual display. Visual display is attractive in every way. Pictures, drawings, or demonstrations add to the visual display. At least four questions are answered. There are minimal or no errors in spelling, punctuation, and grammar. Both buddies can tell about their country without reading the information. Eye contact is maintained. Voices can be heard easily. Both buddies are totally engaged in the task. | |

**Rubric 1.9**

# "Research" Questions on Countries

The following questions might be helpful in getting started with your research. You *do not* have to answer all of them. You and your buddy may select those that are of interest to you. Remember that you will want to give most of the basic facts about your country, even if you only list these facts in a chart. You will also want to find magazine pictures or make drawings to enhance your display.

Where is your country found?

What countries or bodies of water surround your country?

What are the natural resources of your country?

What nationality are the people of your country?

Is there more than one culture to be found in your country?

What is the climate of your country?

What are the products of your country?

What are the physical features of your country?

What is the major language spoken in your country?

What is the major religion in your country?

What is the history of your country?

How does urban life differ from rural life in your country?

What role do the arts and architecture have in your country?

How much of the land of your country is suitable to grow crops?

How do most of the people in your country provide a living?

Do the people of your country have any enemies?

What is the main means of transportation for the people of your country?

Which countries are allies of your country?

What are the politics of your country?

What are the places in your country that tourists would be interested in seeing?

# CONNECTION

# 2

# A New World

## Connections With the Community

Children will benefit from knowing that they are
a part of the community in which they live.
By meeting the members of those various parts,
they will grow in knowledge
and develop a sense of responsibility
for their environment.

# Outcomes of "A New World" Connection

| | |
|---|---|
| While finding information about the moon, students will be reading and writing and communicating with each other. | Being able to plan large endeavors with others gives students the skill they will need in future jobs. | Students will see the beginning of a governmental system as they join a planning commission to create a moon colony. |
| **LITERACY** | **EMPLOYABILITY** | **LIFELONG LEARNING** |
| Students, as members of commissions, will have to draw conclusions based on factual information acquired. They will then make plans using this information. | Researching the needs of the moon colony gives students a look into present and future technology. | Students will learn to work with others as they plan. They will see the value of a compromise as they present issues to others. |
| **PROBLEM SOLVING** | **TECHNOLOGICAL LITERACY** | **PERSONAL/SOCIAL** |
| In researching what people will need to survive on the moon, students must use scientific reasoning to plan the moon colony. | Creating the moon colony gives students the opportunity to be original and use artistic talents. | In planning the moon colony, students will learn people's basic needs for a healthy existence. |
| **MATHEMATIC/SCIENTIFIC REASONING** | **FINE ARTS** | **WELLNESS** |

**Rubric 2.1**

# "A New World" Materials Needed

- **Primary Cycle**

  Books—Moon

  Eggs

  Wrapping

- **Intermediate Cycle**

  Books—Moon

  Paper

  Markers

- **Bonding Cycle**

  Books—Moon

  Milk cartons

  Aluminum foil

  Cardboard tubes

  Clear wrap

  Construction paper

  Boxes

  Glue

  Scissors

  Paper

  Various other materials

# "A New World" Primary Cycle
*Student Task*

## TASK

You have just traveled to the wonderful world of outer space and have had the opportunity to learn many interesting facts about the planets, the sun, and the moon. Someday you may be one of the very first residents of a new and exciting colony on the moon or one of the other planets. The idea is very exciting to you except for one minor problem—you would have to spend the rest of your life eating freeze-dried foods. That idea doesn't excite you at all. You decide to do something about it.

You have decided that an egg would be a good choice to take into space with you, but because of its delicate shell you know you are going to have to protect it. Your job is to design a protective case to hold your egg. It must provide protection from being shaken, having other items placed on top of it, and being dropped from the roof of the school building. If it can stay in one piece, you know it will be able to travel into space with you. You will be scored on the creativity of your design and if it serves the purpose of protecting your egg. Good luck!

## CRITERIA

Creativity of case

Function of case

# "A New World" Primary Cycle
## *Teaching Suggestions*

Young children are fascinated with outer space, supernatural beings, and heroes like Superman and the Star Wars® characters. This teaching unit can be as in-depth as you like. Its main purpose is exposure to facts about the solar system and sparking an interest in the study of space that will encourage a successful bonding activity. There is much available on space study. Gather as much information as you can—*Easy* books, picture books, and more advanced literature—and display them for the children to look at and peak their interest. Also, any teacher supply store should carry posters, mobiles, and other visual displays of the solar system that you may want to purchase.

Start out by asking the students what they know about space, the planets, the moon, space travel, and so on to gain an overview of the knowledge they possess. Explain that this unit gives them the opportunity to travel in space and that they will keep a daily space log of new facts and interesting details they have learned. The space log can be lined or blank paper stapled together with an interesting cover or one the students design on their own. The book should contain enough pages so that each planet gets an individual page or two on which to log information. Each day the students will date it "Stardate _____" using the date when they are making an entry.

To introduce a planet, one of the most entertaining and easily understood books to use as a teaching guide is the *Magic School Bus in Outer Space.* (If it is not available, any other space study book will serve the same purpose.) This book travels from earth through the galaxy, stopping at each planet and offering information about each. It describes what each looks like, its unique characteristics, and if it might be possible to someday live on that planet. The book is entertaining, and children enjoy it while learning important information for their space log. You might also want to use other sources at this time, share pictures of the planet, or use other information you feel your students will benefit from. We suggest studying just one planet a day, discussing it, and then giving the students time to log the new information they have just learned. During the study of the planets, be sure to spend time studying the moon and give the students plenty of information about its surface, environment, and other facts that will aid them with the bonding activity with their buddy. After all of the planets and the moon have been studied, and to add to the enjoyment of the space study, explain the task and rubric. Culminate the study by having a time set aside for the egg case drop. Elicit the help of the school custodian as the official egg dropper!

# Analysis and Reflection: "A New World" Primary Cycle

## STANDARDS: The levels at which students perform the task

| In Progress | Basic | Proficient | Advanced | Comments |
|---|---|---|---|---|
| Purpose of the task is not achieved. | Purpose of the task is somewhat achieved. | Purpose of the task is mostly achieved. | Purpose of the task is totally achieved. | |
| Egg case is unattractive and shows little effort. | Egg case is presentable and shows some effort. | Egg case is attractive and shows effort. | Egg case is appealing and shows great effort. | |
| Egg case shows little thought in design, does not function properly, and does not support self or egg. | Egg case shows some thought and design, does not fully function properly, and supports self but not the egg. | Egg case shows thought and design, functions properly and can be used at least one more time, and supports self but not the egg. | Egg case shows creative thought and original design, is fully functional and reusable, and supports self and egg. | |

Rubric 2.2

44

# "A New World" Intermediate Cycle
## *Student Task*

## TASK

Your community includes the earth and its satellite, the moon. Americans have not only traveled to the moon but have actually walked on its surface. The American flag is planted and waiting for the first people to live there—perhaps you.

To understand how people might live on the moon in years to come, you need to learn as much as you can about the conditions that exist there and how people might be able to survive on its surface.

After conducting an in-depth study of the moon, you need to produce a written record of your findings. The data you discover will be used as a basis for a future buddy activity and is very important to you both. The booklets will then be sent to the children's department of the local library for display and enjoyment.

Your task is to develop a "Book of Moon Facts." To help you in your research, consider the list of questions presented by your teacher. In your collection of data, you will want to have illustrations, graphs, and charts to enhance the meaning and make the information easier to read. Be prepared to share your information with your buddy and anyone in the class who will benefit from the knowledge you have acquired.

## CRITERIA

Data/actual knowledge

Booklet

Presentation to others

# "A New World" Intermediate Cycle
## *Teaching Suggestions*

Boys and girls share the same fascination with outer space. Their natural curiosity makes the introduction of higher-level thinking skills that require application, analysis, and evaluation of factual data an easy and enjoyable experience.

To begin this intermediate activity, start a discussion to discover what students already know about our galaxy. Most will be able to state the names of the planets, some of the constellations, and various other factual data. Showing a video or filmstrip that contains information about the moon will give them a visual picture besides new information. Have students read and take notes for their booklets. If they haven't been introduced to graphing and charting, this is a good time to show them how to organize factual information so that it is easier to read and understand.

It is probably advisable to devote several days to reading and note taking before handing out the rubric. Encourage paired and small-group sharing of information. Your goal is for students to acquire all of the facts that will help them successfully complete the bonding activity that follows.

When the students have a background on the moon, ask them where they think they will live in the future. Relate the growing world population, the environmental problems we face with land, air, and water pollution, and the need for jobs for all citizens. An extension would be to relate the frontier in the westward movement to the frontier of space. Review the basic needs of all humans and ask the students to think about how these needs will be met on a new frontier such as the moon.

When the class has a shared background, hand out the rubrics and the tasks. Explain that the questions are only a guide to thinking about the moon. Emphasize that the booklet they will make needs to be very accurate as it will be a source of reference for the bonding activity that follows.

Contact local space agencies or military posts to see if they would allow students to display both the booklets and the moon colony that will be made. If students are able to use the computer to make their brochures, the appearance will be more professional, but handwritten brochures that exhibit effort are just as effective. An incentive for a high standard would be to select only the best examples for public display. If there are no space agencies available, talk to local libraries and banks who might be willing to display the children's work.

Analysis and Reflection: "A New World" Intermediate Cycle

| | STANDARDS: The levels at which students perform the task | | | |
|---|---|---|---|---|
| In Progress | Basic | Proficient | Advanced | Comments |
| Facts are inaccurate and show no evidence of research. Purpose of the task is not achieved. Facts are difficult to follow and lack organization. Efforts in spelling, punctuation, and grammar interfere with the meaning. Illustrations, graphs, or charts are missing or unrelated to the data. Booklet is unattractive and shows little effort. Student is unable to focus on the project. Student is disruptive while others are working. Student is unable to share information with others. | Some facts might be inaccurate, but there is evidence of research and reading. Purpose of the task is mostly achieved. Facts are understandable, and the order of the presentation does not distract from the information presented. There are some errors in spelling, punctuation, and grammar, but they do not distract from the meaning. Some illustrations, charts, or graphs add to the understanding of the data. Booklet is attractive and shows effort. Student focuses on the task most of the time. Student works without talking excessively. Student shares the information researched. | Most facts are accurate and show evidence of research and reading. Purpose of the task is evident. Facts are generally logical and sequential. Few errors in spelling, punctuation, and grammar do not distract from the meaning. Illustrations, charts, and graphs enhance the understanding of the data. Booklet is attractive and shows effort. Student focuses on the task. Student works without bothering others. Student shares information with others. | All facts are accurate and show evidence of intensive research and reading. Purpose of the task is totally achieved. Facts are presented in a clear, logical, and sequential order. There is evidence of editing, with few or no errors in spelling, punctuation, and grammar. Illustrations, charts, and graphs are detailed and labeled and enhance the understanding of the data. Booklet is appealing in every way and shows great effort. Student stays totally focused on the project and shows great enthusiasm. Student works while sharing new information with others. | |

**Rubric 2.3**

47

# "A New World" Questions to Consider

What is the distance from the earth to the moon?

How much time does it take the moon to travel around the earth?

What is the rotation of the moon?

What is the surface of the moon?

What are the elements found on the moon?

What is the temperature of the moon?

Is there gravity on the moon?

Does the moon have an atmosphere? If so, what does it consist of?

What would man weigh on the moon?

What is the circumference of the moon?

Is there water on the moon?

How long would it take you to travel to the moon by spacecraft? by jet? by car? by bicycle? by walking?

What would a future moon colony need for people to live there successfully?

Include any other information that would be valuable to future space travelers.

# "A New World" Bonding Cycle
## *Student Task*

## TASK

Scientists are preparing plans for people's eventual occupation of the moon. In order to think of every new and innovative idea possible, they have put out a request for help to all children who might one day live on the moon. Now that you have created a booklet of moon data and shared it with your little buddy, you are qualified to answer this call from the world's scientists.

Your task is to create a moon colony where 100 people might one day live. Please remember that every woman, man, and child needs oxygen to breathe, food to eat, water to drink, and a place to live.

To understand your reasoning for including an area or building in the moon colony, it is necessary to become a part of one of the commissions listed below. As a commission member, you first have to discuss the responsibilities of your group and how those plans can be carried out most effectively. Each group must make a list of the essential elements needed to sustain life in a moon colony. (These commissions, their responsibilities, and questions that help to determine needs are available from your teacher.)

Waste Control Management Commission

Air Quality Control Commission

Water Quality Control Commission

Farmers Commission

Building and Business Commission

Transportation Commission

Entertainment/Recreation Commission

After the commissions have determined the needs of the colony, all plans must be submitted to the mayor and the city council for final approval. If the plans are approved, construction on the various parts of the colony can begin. Materials from home will add to the milk cartons, tubes, aluminum foil, clear wrap, construction paper, and cardboard boxes that have already been gathered. Remember that your construction is part of a master plan and must help to meet the needs of the colony as determined by the commissions and the city officials. You should do nothing without first discussing your plans to see how they fit into the moon colony and its needs.

## CRITERIA

Application of knowledge

Visual presentation

Cooperative efforts

# "A New World" Bonding Cycle
## *Teaching Suggestions*

The most difficult part of this activity is encouraging the older buddy to include the ideas, thoughts, and talents of the younger buddy. This project generates a great deal of enthusiasm that can so involve the older students that they forget it is a cooperative effort. It is necessary to devote many class periods to talking, discussing, and planning as a group before any of the construction can begin.

Appoint a mayor pair and four city council pairs to make the final decisions on the moon colony. These students should be ones who can be depended on to work accurately and cooperatively. After these appointments have been made, introduce the various commissions and the responsibilities of each. Explain that each buddy pair needs to be a part of one of the commissions to plan for the necessities of the people who will be inhabiting the moon colony. As commissions meet, plans are finalized, and assignments are made, students must have the approval of the mayor and the city council. This city group is responsible for the master plan that will coordinate all of the constructions, making sure that no area of need is neglected.

As individual buddy pair assignments are made and approved, students can begin to build their constructions. Materials like milk cartons, tubes, aluminum foil, clear wrap, construction paper, and cardboard will aid in the constructions, but don't limit students to these. Encourage them to bring other materials from home to add to the moon colony.

When the constructions are complete, have students explain in writing the purpose of the construction and the need for it in the colony. Remind them that these detailed explanations are very important for viewers of each construction, who will want to understand its purposes.

When the colony is complete, students should prepare an oral presentation of their part in its development. Making a video of the constructions and the students' presentations is one way for parents to share the experience. The video can also be sent to prospective companies who might be willing to display the colony.

# Analysis and Reflection: "A New World" Bonding Cycle

## STANDARDS: The levels at which students perform the task

| In Progress | Basic | Proficient | Advanced | Comments |
|---|---|---|---|---|
| Colony constructions show no consideration for the master plan decided on by members of the class. | Colony constructions provide for some of the needs of the master plan. | Colony constructions are complete and mostly follow the master plan. | Constructions totally provide for people's needs as indicated by the master plan. | |
| Constructions have few or no identifying explanations. | Constructions are labeled with minimal information. | Constructions are labeled and explained. | Constructions are well detailed with complete explanations of their purpose. | |
| There is little or no accurate information applied to the constructions. | Most information is accurate and applies to the needs of the colony. | Accuracy of information is evident. | Information presented is totally accurate. | |
| Project shows little or no higher-level thinking. | Constructions meet the goal of the task but show little evidence of higher-level thinking. | There are few errors in spelling, punctuation, and grammar. | Constructions show evidence of higher-level thinking and planning. | |
| Errors in spelling, punctuation, and grammar interfere with understanding. | There are some errors in spelling, punctuation, and grammar. | Constructions are generally attractive. | There are few or no errors in spelling, punctuation, and grammar. | |
| Constructions have little eye appeal. | Constructions have some eye appeal. | Constructions show effort but lack some detail. | Constructions are appealing in every respect. | |
| There is little or no evidence of effort in the constructions. | Constructions are complete but show limited effort. | Buddies are focused on the task. | Constructions show evidence of great effort. | |
| Buddies are unable to work together and are unfocused. | Buddies focus on the task without much talking. | Both buddies contribute ideas to the task and are able to work together cooperatively. | Both buddies are totally focused on the task. | |
| Buddies are loud, and talking interferes with others in class. | Buddies work together some of the time but mostly work individually. | | Buddies work together, sharing ideas and discussing as they work. | |
| | | | Big buddy encourages little buddy. | |

**Rubric 2.4**

# "A New World" Job Descriptions

## MAYOR

Your job is to be in charge of the master plan of the moon colony. You must be aware of all of the needs of the people who will be living in the colony. You must be sure that the commissions have planned for every element of community living because the colony must be self-sustaining. Some products can be brought from earth, but the majority of things needed must come from the colony itself. This means that the colony must provide enough water, food, and places to live and a waste disposal system for everyone in the community. You and the city council will give the final approval to the plans made by the various commissions. If you do not see the need for certain constructions, you must use your veto power to send the members of the commission back to replan. Don't be afraid to ask them to justify how the construction they've planned will benefit all of the people in the moon colony.

### *Questions to Consider*

- **Waste Control**

  Where will garbage be stored?

  How will garbage be disposed?

  How will human waste be disposed?

  How will garbage be collected?

  Who will be in charge of disposing waste?

  Will there be special machines to take care of waste?

  Will waste be recycled?

  Will there be laws to govern waste disposal?

  What will happen to violators?

  Other questions that might arise

- **Air Quality**

  Because there is no way that people can breathe on the moon, how will oxygen be provided?

  Will oxygen be provided to each person, or will there be one way of providing oxygen for the whole colony?

  How will pollutants in the air be disposed?

  Will there be restrictions on factories?

  Who will monitor air quality?

  Will each place of residence have a separate means of air control, or will there be one place that keeps track of air quality?

  What will happen when there is not enough air for the people in the moon colony to breathe?

  What emergency measures will be taken?

  Will there be laws to govern air quality?

  Other questions that might arise

- **Water**

  How will drinking water be obtained for every person in the colony?

  How will water be obtained for bathing, washing clothes, and maintenance of machines or factories?

  How will water be provided to any livestock on the moon?

  Will water be used for recreation?

  Will water be recycled?

  Will there be laws governing the use of water?

  Who will be in charge of water control?

  What will happen if there is not enough water?

  What emergency plans will be taken until more water can be acquired?

  Other questions that might arise

- **Farming**

  How will land be used?

  Where will soil for growing crops come from?

  How much land will be set aside for farming and ranching?

  What crops will be grown?

  What livestock will be ranched?

  Will families have gardens?

What fruits, vegetables, and meats will be needed by the people?

Will there be alternative ways of creating food?

How will products be sold and distributed?

Will there be laws about farming?

Who will farm and ranch?

Other questions that might arise

- **Buildings and Businesses**

What kind of housing will be available for the people on the moon colony?

What kinds of business buildings will be allowed?

Will there be a limit to the levels of a building?

Who will be in charge of new constructions?

What materials will be used for construction?

Who will build new constructions?

Are there any laws controlling building?

Will there be heating and cooling in the constructions?

Other questions that might arise

- **Transportation**

How will people on the moon colony travel from place to place in the colony?

Will there be mass transportation? If so, what kind?

Will there be individual transportation? If so, what kind?

How will colonists go back and forth between the colony and earth?

Will there be laws about transportation?

Who will be in charge of transportation?

How much will transportation cost?

Other questions that might arise

- **Entertainment/Recreation**

What kinds of entertainment will be available?

Will there be parks?

Who will be in charge of the maintenance of parks?

Will there be sports?

Will sports games be played?

Will there be water sports?

How will entertainment be produced?

Who will be in charge of entertainment and recreation?

Will there be laws about entertainment and recreation?

How much will entertainment and recreation cost, and who will pay for it?

Other questions that might arise

## WASTE CONTROL MANAGEMENT

Your job is to consider all of the ways to control waste. Thinking about the waste that America produces in the form of garbage, sewage, and pollution, you must decide how these same problems will be handled in the moon colony. Your job is to govern the use of water and decide what the consequences will be for those who do not obey the laws. You need to determine how much water will be allotted for farming and ranching and provide emergency plans for any occasion when water might be scarce. Finally, you need to present your plans to the mayor and all of the other commissioners for approval.

### Questions to Consider

How will garbage be collected?

Where will garbage be stored?

How will garbage be disposed?

How will human waste be disposed?

Who will be in charge of disposing waste?

Will there be special machines to take care of waste?

Will waste be recycled?

Will there be laws to govern waste disposal?

What will happen to violators?

Other questions that might arise

## AIR QUALITY MANAGEMENT

Your job is to decide how oxygen will be provided for people living in the moon colony. You must establish the level of desired air quality, considering such things as factory pollutants, what materials can be burned, what plants grown, and so on. Remember, life will cease without oxygen to breathe. Your responsibility is enormous. Do your job well.

## Questions to Consider

Because there is no way that people can breathe on the moon, how will oxygen be provided?

Will oxygen be provided to each person, or will there be one way of providing oxygen for the whole colony?

How will pollutants in the air be disposed?

Will there be pollution restrictions placed on factories?

Who will monitor air quality?

Will each place of residence have a separate means of air control, or will there be one place that keeps track of air quality?

What will happen when there is not enough air for the people in the moon colony to breathe?

What emergency measures will be taken?

Will there be laws to govern air quality?

Other questions that might arise

## WATER COMMISSION

Your responsibility is to provide water for every person, plant, and animal in the moon colony. Remember, all living things must have water to survive. Water is also needed for bathing, cleaning, and maintenance of factories and businesses. You have to decide if the scarce and precious water will be available for recreation, such as swimming or boating, and how to recycle the water. You need to decide how to handle emergencies and who will make final decisions. Your job is vital to the continuation of the moon colony. Plan carefully.

## Questions to Consider

How will drinking water be obtained for every person in the colony?

How will water be obtained for bathing, washing clothes, and maintaining machines or factories?

How will water be provided to any livestock on the moon?

Will water be used for recreation?

Will water be recycled?

Will there be laws governing the use of water?

Who will be in charge of water control?

What will happen if there is not enough water?

Will there be emergency plans for providing water until more can be acquired?

Other questions that might arise

## FARMERS COMMISSION

Your job is to decide how many acres of the moon colony will be used for farming and ranching. This is not an easy job because you have to provide enough food for everyone in the colony. Remember people's needs for fruits, vegetables, grains, milk, and meats. You must decide who will be in charge of the food we need and how it will be distributed. You also need to make laws governing what individuals can produce because not only the land but also the water and air will be affected with more growth. Finally, you must make a master plan to present to the mayor and the other commissioners for final approval.

### Questions to Consider

How will land be used?

Where will soil for growing crops come from?

How much land will be set aside for farming and ranching?

What crops will be grown?

What livestock will be ranched?

Will families have gardens?

What fruits, vegetables, and meats will be needed by the people?

Will there be alternative ways of creating food?

How will products be sold and distributed?

Will there be laws about farming?

Who will farm and ranch?

Other questions that might arise

## BUILDING AND BUSINESS COMMISSION

Your job is to decide what buildings will be allowed in the moon colony. You must decide whether people will live in multifamily housing or individual housing, what the housing will be made of, and if it will be a part of the moon environment. You must decide what businesses are needed to sustain people in the colony and where their buildings will be located and how tall they can be. You must decide if there will be a limit to the number of buildings that can be constructed and how constructions will be recycled and repaired. You must decide how dwellings will be heated and cooled or if they even need to be. You must decide where you will obtain materials for building and how much building will cost. You must make laws about building and consequences for those who do not obey the laws. Finally, you must prepare a plan for buildings and housing that will be within the limits of the colony yet provide for all of its needs. Be prepared to present this plan to the mayor and the other commissioners for final approval.

### *Questions to Consider*

> What kind of housing will be available for the people on the moon colony?
>
> What kinds of business buildings will be allowed?
>
> Will there be a limit to the levels of a building?
>
> Who will be in charge of new constructions?
>
> Where will materials be found for use in construction?
>
> Who will build new constructions?
>
> Are there any laws controlling building?
>
> Will there be heating and cooling in the constructions?
>
> Other questions that might arise

## TRANSPORTATION COMMISSION

Your job is to provide the transportation for all persons in the moon colony. You must decide if there will be mass transportation or individual transportation, and then what each will be. You must decide how the colonists will travel from the moon colony to Earth and other planets. You must decide how the colony will receive items from Earth that it needs to survive. You must decide who will maintain the transportation, how much it will cost, and who will run it. You must consider the machinery needed to build your transportation and where the materials for development and maintenance will be obtained. Consider the size of the moon colony and the number of colonists. Remember, they will have to be able to get to jobs, shops, and recreation. You also need to create both the laws to protect any means of transportation and the consequences for those who break those laws. Finally, you need to draw an overview of your ideas to present to the mayor and the other commissioners for final approval.

### Questions to Consider

How will people on the moon colony travel from place to place in the colony?

Will there be mass transportation? If so, what kind?

Will there be individual transportation? If so, what kind?

How will colonists go back and forth between the colony and earth?

Will there be laws about transportation?

Who will be in charge of transportation?

How much will transportation cost?

Other questions that might arise

## ENTERTAINMENT/RECREATION COMMISSION

Your job is to decide how the moon colonists will entertain themselves. You must decide if there will be parks, sports facilities, swimming, fishing, and so on. This is not easy because you must consider the amount of land that each activity will use, the amount of vegetation required, and the air and water needed to maintain the area. You must decide if there will be organized games or individual means of entertainment. You must determine the materials that you will need for your entertainment and recreation and where those materials will come from. Remember that the colonists will not be able to leave the moon colony often, and they must have activities that will consume their leisure time. Be creative in your thinking. You might want to consider various age levels and ability levels. Do not be limited to what we now know. You also need to create both the laws that govern areas of recreation and the consequences for those who do not obey those laws. Finally, create an overall plan to present to the mayor and the other commissioners for final approval. Remember that you might need to justify your plans as many essential needs must be considered by the city council before those of entertainment and recreation.

### Questions to Consider

What kinds of entertainment will be available?

Will there be parks?

Who will be in charge of the maintenance of parks?

Will there be sports?

Will sports games be played?

Will there be water sports?

How will entertainment be produced?

Who will be in charge of entertainment and recreation?

Will there be laws about entertainment and recreation?

How much will entertainment and recreation cost, and who will pay for it?

Other questions that might arise

# "A New World" Suggested Books

| | |
|---|---|
| *Space Exploration* | Anita McCormick |
| *The Moon and You* | E. C. Krupp |
| *Richie's Rocket* | Joan Anderson |
| *Space* | Christoper Maynard |
| *The Mice on the Moon* | Rodney Peppe |
| *What's Out There?* | Lynn Wilson |
| *Spacey Riddles* | Katy Hall |
| *To the Moon and Beyond* | [Video recording] |
| *Our Future in Space* | Don Berliner |
| *The Golden Book of Space Exploration* | Diana Mocha |
| *Mission to the Planets* | Patrick More |
| *Moon Walk: The First Trip to the Moon* | Judy Donnelly |
| *Junk in Space* | Richard Maurer |
| *The Magic Moon Machine* | Jane Moncure |
| *Going to the Moon* | James Muirden |
| *Space Mission Problem Solving* | Software; Orange Cherry, $39.00 |
| *Science Adventure* | Software; Knowledge Adventure, $42.95 |
| *Space Adventure* | Software; Knowledge Adventure, $42.95 |
| *Space Shuttle Word Problems* | Software; Orange Cherry, $39.95 |

# CONNECTION

# 3

# Math Is a Game

---

### Problem Solving

Man and woman stand above all other living creatures
because they have superior intelligence.
Each can construct knowledge and meaning
from his or her environment
by becoming an active problem solver
in the events of the world.

### Mathematical Thinking

Too often, children are not aware
of mathematics in their lives.
Too often, mathematics is thought of as
hours of drudgery and repetition.
What better way to learn thinking,
multiples, and addition than through
a friendly game!
Everyone involved has a good time,
and new family interests are developed.

# Outcomes of "Math Is a Game" Connection

**LITERACY**

In writing game directions for an audience, students practice reading, writing, and editing skills.

**PROBLEM SOLVING**

Students are able to combine knowledge of existing games with math skills to create a new game.

**MATHEMATIC/SCIENTIFIC REASONING**

Students develop criteria and rules for the game that are without error.

**EMPLOYABILITY**

Students learn to find answers to authentic problems. Game planning parallels planning in the workforce.

**TECHNOLOGICAL LITERACY**

Students are able to use calculators and the computer to practice and create new games.

**FINE ARTS**

Design of game boards for eye appeal, originality, and neatness use students' artistic skills.

**LIFELONG LEARNING**

Being able to choose a course of action while considering alternatives is a lifelong, important skill.

**PERSONAL/SOCIAL**

Learning to cooperate with others is a skill that students will need in the workforce.

**Rubric 3.1**

# "Math Is a Game" Materials Needed

- **Primary Cycle**

  Various games

- **Intermediate Cycle**

  Dominoes

  Paper

  Multiplication charts, optional

  Calculators, optional

- **Bonding Cycle**

  Paper

  Pencil

  Dice

  Attribute blocks, if available

  Spinners

  Cubes

  Tag board

  Markers

  Any other math materials available

# "Math Is a Game" Primary Cycle
*Student Task*

## TASK

In several weeks, our grade level will host an open house for the students in the grade below us. There will be a lot of activities going on that day that will help us share with the youngsters what our grade is all about. Because cooperating and getting along with others is such an important thing to learn at school, a game center will be set up to teach those important skills. Our class has been chosen to work the game area.

Here's what you are to do. Choose a game that you enjoy playing, one we've learned at school or one you have at home. Learn how to play the game well, know the directions, and be able to explain the directions to anyone who may want to play the game with you. You will be scored on how well you teach the game and how well you get along with others in your group.

## CRITERIA

Cooperative play

Staying on task

Learning and teaching a game

# "Math Is a Game" Primary Cycle
## *Teaching Suggestions*

Learning to play simple board games, card games, and dominoes in the early primary grades can teach students to learn cooperation, academic skills, and higher-level thinking skills. However, many students today have very little knowledge of how to play games. They know Nintendo, Sega, and videogames, but very few know dominoes or the board game Chutes and Ladders and the strategies to win at tic-tac-toe. Early in the school year, gather as many children's games as you can. (Yard sales, newspaper classified ads, and thrift stores are places where you may find many for a small price.) Introduce the games by showing the game parts and explaining their function. Explain the strategy of each game and the directions. It is then a good idea to model the game, choosing several students to play the game with you. Have the entire class sit in a semicircle around the game board and begin to play. While playing, talk through what may be taking place and why a certain move might have been made. Be careful not to give away too many strategies as this is what you want the students to be able to do on their own when they get to know the game better. After several sessions of introducing games and modeling them, allot time for the students to play the games on their own. This is a good time to explain to them that winning the game is not the most important thing, that playing with friends and having fun is much more important. The use of a MORE OR LESS spinner (common in all Math Their Way games) alleviates the competition of winning and puts the focus back on having fun. (The goal behind the spinner is that each child keeps track of how many games he or she has won, and before cleaning up, the spinner is spun and depending on where it falls, more or less, that person is the overall winner.) After exposure to the games, the students should be ready to proceed with the task. You may have to schedule a time with a lower-grade teacher to ensure that the task is as authentic as possible.

# Analysis and Reflection: "Math Is A Game" Primary Cycle

**STANDARDS: The levels at which students perform the task**

| In Progress | Basic | Proficient | Advanced | Comments |
|---|---|---|---|---|
| Student shows no interest in learning games. | Student shows some interest in learning games. | Student shows interest and enjoyment in learning games. | Student demonstrates enjoyment in learning games. | |
| Student cannot stay on task. | Student can stay on task for short periods of time. | Student can stay on task until completion of game. | Student verbalizes pleasure from playing games. | |
| Student fidgets, loses interest, and is argumentative. | Student seems distracted, loses concentration, and can be argumentative at times. | Student shows cooperation. | Student can stay focused on task and keep others on task. | |
| Student cannot teach others how to play the game. | Student can teach the game by playing it but not by explaining the directions. | Student can teach the game by playing it and is able to explain simple directions. | Student is cooperative and makes playing the game enjoyable for others. | |
| | | | Student can teach the game by explaining all the directions and adapting directions to make it easier and more understandable. | |

**Rubric 3.2**

# "Math Is a Game" Intermediate Cycle
## *Student Task*

## TASK

Your teacher has told you that you will be having a very important multiplication test next week. She has suggested that since you already know how to play dominoes using multiples of 5 that one "fun" way to practice and study at the same time would be to play dominoes using different multiples. If you need to study 8s, for instance, then you could score by accumulating 8, 16, or 24 points. If you need to study 7s, then you would need to have a total of 7, 14, or 21 points. If you have practiced and feel that you have mastered dominoes with the different multiples, then, with your group, create another game that would help your classmates learn their multiplication tables. Use the dominoes in any manner that makes sense and provides practice. Be ready to share your ideas with your classmates.

## CRITERIA

Math skills

Cooperative efforts

Creativity and higher-level thinking

# "Math Is a Game" Intermediate Cycle
*Teaching Suggestions*

The use of dominoes is a great way to teach intermediate students multiples and mental math addition. Begin by modeling the thinking process required in playing the game. In the real game, multiples of 5 are used to score. Because the 5s are familiar to the majority of students, it's a good scoring multiple to begin with. Once the students have become familiar with the game, they should play for several sessions. Explain the scoring sheet and how you would like each student to try to use mental math when adding the scores each round. If students need more assistance, suggest that they use a multiplication chart or even a calculator. However, even this will need to be modeled.

When students are comfortable with scoring using multiples of 5, challenge them to play using other multiples. This activity is one that can be played throughout the year. It is better to skip days rather than playing every day. Too much of anything can get boring!

Dominoes is also a good game for students to play when they finish their work or on those long winter days when the weather dictates indoor recess. When you wish to evaluate the students' performances, hand out the rubric and hold a conference.

Analysis and Reflection: "Math Is a Game" Intermediate Cycle

## STANDARDS: The levels at which students perform the task

| In Progress | Basic | Proficient | Advanced | Comments |
|---|---|---|---|---|
| Student must constantly refer to the multiplication chart and, for the most part, merely matches dominoes in one-to-one correspondence. | Student knows some of the multiplication tables and can recognize multiples to score. | Student knows the majority of the multiplication chart and can discern choices for scoring. | Student knows multiplication tables and can select plays to acquire the highest scores. | |
| Student can add only by counting or using the calculator. | Student can add by writing down the problem. | Student can generally add mentally and correctly. | Student is able to add mentally and correctly. | |
| There is little or no evidence of higher-level thinking. | Student has limited ability to play using strategy and higher-level thinking skills. | Student shows some evidence of higher-level thinking while playing. | Student shows evidence of higher-level thinking while playing. | |
| Group is unfocused on the task and talks and plays. | Group is working but talking. | Group is focused on the task for most of the time allotted, but some talk interferes with the game. | Group is completely focused on the task. | |
| Group members argue and do not listen to each other. | Group members cooperate with each other to some extent. | Group members cooperate in helping each other achieve the task. | Group members listen and discuss cooperatively. | |
| Students make no attempt to create a game using dominoes to practice math facts. | Students try to create a game using dominoes to practice multiplication tables. | Group creates a game that gives partial practice with multiplication. | Group creates a game to practice multiplication. | |
| | Some parts of the game are understandable. | Game is mostly understandable. | Game is completely and easily understood. | |

**Rubric 3.3**

71

# "Math Is a Game" Intermediate Cycle
*Dominoes Score Sheet*

Players:


Scoring Using
  Multiples of      2     3     4     5     6     7     8     9     (circle one)

Player


_____


Player


_____


Player


_____


Player


_____


**Figure 3.1**

# "Math Is a Game" Bonding Cycle
## *Student Task*

## TASK

Math is the ability to have number sense. It also includes the ability to see patterns, take measurements, understand geometry, estimate, generalize, and justify. Using these skills and processes, people can find answers to authentic problems that confront them each day in both the home and the workplace.

The task for you and your buddy is to create a series of math games that will teach your classmates how much fun math can be. You can use any math materials that are available: dice, playing cards, tiles, cubes, dominoes, attribute blocks, and so on. If you like, create your own materials. You can make board games, memory games, or problem-solving games. Your games can be simple or complex. (Thinking of other games that you have played might give you other ideas to model after.) Remember that you will need to be able to write the rules for the game and teach it to other buddies and, perhaps, to other children in the school, maybe even to senior citizen buddies in a nursing home.

## CRITERIA

The game

Higher-level thinking

Cooperative efforts

# "Math Is a Game" Bonding Cycle
## *Teaching Suggestions*

Before you begin this bonding activity, you will hopefully have given your students ample experiences with math games. These game experiences will serve as models as the students create original games.

Hand out the task and the rubric to the buddy pairs. Point out the math materials you have available, the poster boards, and various other things that you think will inspire students to think mathematically. Buddy pairs will need time to explore and experiment with their ideas before actually writing the rules for their game or designing the pieces for their games. Give them as long as they need. Good ideas come from planning and talking together.

Once an idea begins to take form, the students need to write a first draft of what they are doing and try out what they are thinking. If they feel pretty sure that their game will work, they should try the game on other buddy pairs. If any errors exist, they will probably be found in this first experimental stage. If students are creating a game board it is probably better to have them draw a plan before actually handing out the poster board. (You always have those who jump in head first without being sure there is water in the pool!)

If buddy pairs are feeling quite lost, hand out the Game Form provided in the lesson. This is more concrete and may help them get started. In fact, you may want to start the entire group out with the form for the first game they create. You will know the abilities and the confidence level of your students.

Finally, remind the students that they need to write out a final set of rules to be included with the game. (If computers are available for your use, these rules could be keyed in and printed out. It would also be very exciting for students to create their games for the computer!)

Use the student games for the classroom or take them to other students in other classes. If a nursing home is close by, ask permission to bring in the students and their games for an afternoon of playing with the senior buddies. Both the residents and your students will benefit from the experience. Parents might also enjoy a game night where students present their games and then play with family and friends.

Analysis and Reflection: "Math Is a Game" Bonding Cycle

**STANDARDS: The levels at which students perform the task**

| In Progress | Basic | Proficient | Advanced | Comments |
|---|---|---|---|---|
| Purpose of the task is not achieved. | Purpose of the project is achieved. | Purpose of the task is evident in games. | Both buddies attempt to listen and discuss. | |
| Game is incomplete and/or incorrect. | Game is mostly complete and correct. | Game is complete and correct. | Purpose of the task is totally achieved. | |
| Game directions are difficult to follow and lack organization. | Game directions are understandable, and the order does not take away from the game. | Game directions are mostly logical and sequential. | Game is well detailed, complete, and correct. | |
| Game is minimal. Errors in spelling, punctuation, and grammar interfere with the meaning. | Game is adequate. | Game is interesting. | Game directions are clear, logical, and in sequential order. | |
| Game shows no higher-level thinking skills. | There are some errors in spelling, punctuation, and grammar, but they do not interfere with the meaning. | Few errors in spelling, punctuation, and grammar do not take away from the meaning. | Game is appealing in every aspect. | |
| Buddies are unfocused on making the game. | Game shows more of the lower-level thinking skill. | Game includes some of the higher-level thinking skills. | Directions show evidence of editing, with few or no errors in spelling, punctuation, and grammar. | |
| Buddies are loud, with too much talking and playing. | Both buddies achieve the task, but talking does interfere at times. | Buddies are focused on the task the majority of the time. | Game includes the majority of the higher-level thinking skills. | |
| Buddies do not listen to each other and/or argue with each other. | Big buddy does the majority of game making. | Both buddies contribute to making the game, but the big buddy may be in charge. | Both buddies are completely focused on the task. | |
| | Buddies each do a part of the game, with much planning or discussion. | | Both buddies contribute their ideas and talents. | |
| | | | Both buddies listen, discuss, and plan in a mannerly way. | |

**Rubric 3.4**

# "Math Is a Game" Game Form

Name of the Game

Number of Players

Materials Needed to Play the Game

Object of the Game

Rules for the Game

How to Begin the Game

Skills the Game Teaches

**Figure 3.2**

# "Math Is a Game" Suggested Books

| | |
|---|---|
| *Cooperative Learning in Math* | Bob Bernstein |
| *Numbers Count* | Bob Bernstein |
| *Thinking Numbers: Math Games and Activities* | Bob Bernstein |
| *Math Fun With Money Puzzlers* | Rose Wyler |
| *Counting* | Lakshmi Hewavisenti |
| *Shapes and Solids* | Lakshmi Hewavisenti |
| *Problem Solving* | Lakshmi Hewavisenti |
| *Anno's Math Games* | Mitsumasa Anno |
| *Anno's Math Games 111* | Mitsumasa Anno |
| *More Brain Boosters: Projects and Games* | Dana McMillan |
| *Games for Math* | Peggy Kaye |
| *Math and Logic Games* | Franco Agostini |
| *More Numbers* | Lalie Harcourt |
| *The Good Apple Math Book* | Gary Grimm |
| *Math, Writing and Games in the Classroom* | Herbert Kohl |
| *Math Gems: Sparkling Activities* | Carole Greenes |
| *Hands on Math, Vols. 1-3* | Software; Ventura Education System, no price |
| *Talking Money* | Software; Orange Cherry, $48.95 |
| *Talking Clock* | Software; Orange Cherry, $48.95 |

# CONNECTION

# 4

# P.S. Write Back Soon

## Letter Writing

Receiving a letter in the mail with news from
family members or friends can be so exciting!
A thank-you note for your efforts or an invitation
can make you feel so appreciated.
A business letter, a fax,
or a computer message can be so informative.
A letter from the past can connect you with the past.
Young people need to be aware of the
many forms of letter writing
and their impact on all who share them.

# Outcomes of "P.S. Write Back Soon" Connection

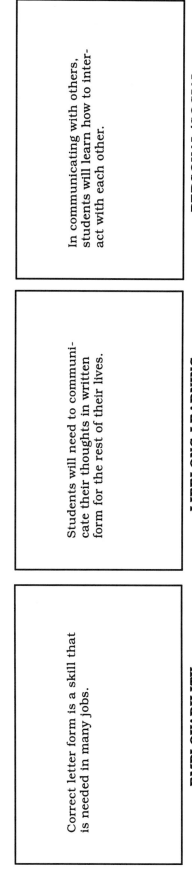

**MATHEMATIC/SCIENTIFIC REASONING**

As they write to one another, students will see how we are all dependent on one another.

**PROBLEM SOLVING**

Letter writing lets students decide how to present their thoughts in the most understandable way.

**LITERACY**

To write a letter and receive a letter, students must be able to read, write, and listen to the words of others.

**PERSONAL/SOCIAL**

In communicating with others, students will learn how to interact with each other.

**LIFELONG LEARNING**

Students will need to communicate their thoughts in written form for the rest of their lives.

**EMPLOYABILITY**

Correct letter form is a skill that is needed in many jobs.

**Rubric 4.1**

79

# "P.S. Write Back Soon" Materials Needed

- **Primary Cycle**
  Books—Letter writing
  Colored markers

- **Intermediate Cycle**
  Folktales

- **Bonding Cycle**
  Paper
  Envelopes
  Mail boxes, optional
  Mail bags, optional
  Stamp pad and stamps

# "P.S. Write Back Soon" Primary Cycle
## *Student Task*

## TASK

Letter writing can be fun, and receiving a letter through the mail is even more fun. Some companies that make products especially for young children love receiving letters from children telling them what they like or dislike about their products. Many of these companies respond by sending back coupons or free samples of their products.

Your job is to write a letter to one of the companies listed on the board. In your letter you are to tell them who you are, how old you are, and what you think of the product they sell. You must also include why you feel as you do. For example, if you are writing to the makers of Kid Cuisine you might want to tell them why you like or dislike their chicken nugget dinner. Remember, you are writing to an audience, so you will be scored on correct letter form and content of your letter. You may receive assistance from a friend or from the teacher.

## CRITERIA

Correct letter form
Content/ideas

# "P.S. Write Back Soon" Primary Cycle
## *Teaching Suggestions*

This activity is used at the beginning of the school year and thereafter as a reminder to primary students, whose assignment is to keep a daily diary. To help them understand what a diary is, share the story *Kitty Cat's Diary* (see suggested book list for an alternative if this book is not available). Follow this with a discussion on the important parts of Kitty's entries: the date, opening, entry, closing, and picture. Then demonstrate a diary entry with different colored markers to highlight each area of the entry. Next, distribute the diaries (a spiral notebook, plain or lined paper stapled together) and encourage students to make an entry. Writing should be encouraged, but accept pictures if that is all the student feels comfortable with. The following day, reread several entries from Kitty's diary, after which the students will write another entry.

Once they have made several entries and seem to be feeling comfortable with the required elements of a diary entry, introduce them to letter writing. Share a brief letter you may have received in the mail or, if available, read *The Jolly Postman* to them. Do a compare-and-contrast (same/different) chart in which the students compare a diary entry to a letter. This exercise points out that many of the same elements needed for their diary are needed in a letter. It is a good idea at this time to write a group letter—say, to the PE teacher, the music teacher, or another class in the school—to point out the key elements of letter writing and how the focus changes from the personal, informal approach taken in a diary entry to the more formal, informative, and inquisitive approach taken in a letter. Immediately following this activity explain the task and rubric to the students. Keep in mind that younger students may need some assistance with this task because of its emphasis on writing.

Analysis and Reflection: "P.S. Write Back Soon" Primary Cycle

| In Progress | Basic | Proficient | Advanced | Comments |
|---|---|---|---|---|
| **STANDARDS: The levels at which students perform the task** | | | | |
| Letters show no correct letter form. | Some parts of the letter form are used. | Letter mostly uses correct letter form. | Letter is written in correct letter form. | |
| Student communicates meaning through pictures and print. | Student communicates by experimenting with print, using beginning and ending sounds. | Student understands that writing has meaning and purpose. | Student uses a correct form to convey meaning. | |
| Random letters—a string of letters—are used. | Simple sentences are used. | Ideas are stated in an orderly fashion. | Student develops an organizational plan. | |
| Environmental print is included in the string of letters. | The same idea is stated over and over. | Descriptive words are used. | Sophisticated sentences are used. | |
| | No plan is evident. | Topic is expressed in multiple sentences. | Descriptive words and phrases are used. | |
| | | Student is able to communicate through a letter. | There is beginning evidence of a writer's feelings. | |

**Rubric 4.2**

# "P.S. Write Back Soon" Intermediate Cycle
## *Student Task*

## TASK

Letter writing is becoming a lost art, but it shouldn't! There is nothing more exciting than to run to the mailbox to find a letter addressed to you from a special friend. Your task is to write letters as though you were a folktale character, such as Cinderella, to another folktale character, such as Snow White. One of your classmates can be one of the characters, and you can be the other. You will want to think about the things that each character has experienced and then write letters back and forth as though the two were really the best of friends but always staying in the role of the folktale character.

Because you are writing to an audience, your letters have to be in correct letter form. You will need to edit for spelling, punctuation, and grammar errors, too. This will be an enjoyable assignment, but the letters will be assessed using the rubric.

## CRITERIA

Ability to stay in character

Correct letter form

Mechanics

# "P.S. Write Back Soon" Intermediate Cycle
## *Teaching Suggestions*

Begin by encouraging students to read folklore. Discuss the characters found in the different stories and how we know them as people. Set up situations that give the characters reasons to talk with each other. For example, Snow White might want to know where Cinderella got the dress that she wore to the ball. Suggest that students act out what they might say to each other before they begin writing. Students always enjoy this relaxed, unassessed part of the assignment.

When it is time to begin the actual letters, have another adult assist you. Put a large sheet of paper in a place where everyone can see it. Each of you select a folklore character and ask each other questions, which you write down. Using two different colors of markers will help the students see what each of the characters is saying. If you are the Wolf in *Little Red Riding Hood,* you might ask Humpty Dumpty if he would like to come to dinner. If you are one of the Three Little Pigs, you might ask Sleeping Beauty how she was able to grow such a thick hedge around her castle. Use your imagination—the more outrageous the better. The students will love it!

After you have modeled, hand out large sheets of paper to pairs of students. Each assumes a folklore character and asks questions of each other, answering the way the character in the tale would answer. The rule that makes this an exciting activity is that there is no talking, only writing.

Present the Letter Form to the students and, if available, read *The Jolly Postman* or other letter books to the class. Remind the children of the conversations between characters that they have already had. Hand out the rubric and explain that this assignment will be assessed.

Analysis and Reflection: "P.S. Write Back Soon" Intermediate Cycle

## STANDARDS: The levels at which students perform the task

| In Progress | Basic | Proficient | Advanced | Comments |
|---|---|---|---|---|
| Letters are incomplete and/or use incorrect letter form. Letters are difficult to follow and lack organization. Accuracy of information about folktale characteristics is questionable. Errors in spelling, punctuation, and grammar interfere with the meaning. Letters become third-person narratives. Letters have no paragraphs and no transition. Letters are not creative or original. | Letters have some details and are mostly correct in form. Letters are understandable, and order does not take away from the meaning. Accuracy of information about folktale characteristics is limited. Some errors in spelling, punctuation, and grammar do not interfere with the meaning. Letters attempt to stay in character and use the first person some of the time. Letters have paragraphs but no transition. The letters are acceptable but not very original. | Letters are detailed and in correct form. Letters are clear, and the order is logical and sequential. Information about folktale characteristics is mostly accurate. There are few errors in spelling, punctuation, and grammar. Letters stay in character and use the first person the majority of the time. Letters have paragraphs and use some transition. Letters show some creativity and originality. | Letters are detailed, complete, and in correct form. Letters are very clear, logical, and in sequential order. Accuracy of information about folktale characteristics is total. There is evidence of editing, with minimal or no errors in spelling, punctuation, and grammar. Letters are written as the selected characters using the first person always. Letters have paragraphs with effective use of transition. Letters show extensive originality and creativity. | |

**Rubric 4.3**

86

# "P.S. Write Back Soon" Intermediate Cycle
## *Letter Form*

_____

_____

_____

_____

-------------------------------------------------------------

- - - - - - - - - - - - - - - - - - - - - - - - - - - - - - - - -

- - - - - - - - - - - - - - - - - - - - - - - - - - - - - - - - -

- - - - - - - - - - - - - - - - - - - - - - - - - - - - - - - - -

- - - - - - - - - - - - - - - - - - - - - - - - - - - - - - - - -

- - - - - - - - - - - - - - - - - - - - - - - - - - - - - - - - -

- - - - - - - - - - - - - - - - - - - - - - - - - - - - - - - - -

- - - - - - - - - - - - - - - - - - - - - - - - - - - - - - - - -

- - - - - - - - - - - - - - - - - - - - - - - - - - - - - - - - -

- - - - - - - - - - - - - - - - - - - - - - - - - - - - - - - - -

_____

_____

**Figure 4.1**

# "P.S. Write Back Soon" Bonding Cycle
## *Student Task*

## TASK

People communicate with others daily through the written word. These communications may be for personal, business, entertainment, or information uses. The United States Post Office delivers millions of these types of letters each day. You and your buddy have done an extensive study of letter writing and what makes a quality letter. You are now ready to use your knowledge to educate the rest of the students in the school.

You and your buddy will be a part of a schoolwide postal system providing mail to each classroom and student on a daily basis.

The postal jobs vary and require the work of talented and dedicated people. Study the job descriptions provided and decide how your talents fit the needs of any of the positions. Decide which job you and your buddy would like to perform. Remember, you will be working as a team at that job, so find the one that best fits your skills as a team. You are required to fill out an application, take a short postal exam, and have a personal interview. How well you and your buddy prepare the application and perform on the exam and during the interview will determine whether or not you receive a position for this quarter. Be sure to discuss this with your buddy and come to some agreement before you submit your application. You will be notified when your interview is scheduled.

## CRITERIA

Cooperative efforts

# "P.S. Write Back Soon" Bonding Cycle
## *Teaching Suggestions*

Before beginning this activity, it is important to inform fellow staff members that a schoolwide postal system will be placed in service. You may want to address the entire staff at a meeting by securing at least 15 minutes on the agenda to inform them that you want to provide the students with a real-life experience in which they apply basic skills: addressing envelopes, writing a letter using appropriate punctuation, locating street addresses, and using ZIP codes. The desired outcome is to unite the entire student body through a student-centered, schoolwide communication system. Point out that teachers' support is needed in their classrooms to provide students with the skills needed to use the postal system successfully: proper letter form, addressing envelopes, and so on. Explain that students will name the post office and choose street names, addresses, and ZIP codes for each room in the building; a list of all important information will be posted in each classroom for easy reference. (This could be an individual decision, as you may want each class and the teacher to decide on a street name and a ZIP code for their room.)

Following the teacher orientation, it is time to explain the postal system to the group of students that will be responsible throughout the year for its operation. A good way to begin is to ask the students to tell you everything they know about the post office, its operation, or anything specific about its functioning. List their responses. After they have had the opportunity to tell what they know, set up a field trip to your local postal outlet. The postal outlets in any city or town are very receptive to taking students on tours through their facilities and providing information about their jobs. After the tour, hold a discussion to talk about what they saw and learned. Again, list all student responses. Then distribute the list of postal vocabulary and meanings included in this unit. The students may have mentioned a topic but did not know the precise terminology, so this list provides them with the proper terms to use with each other while on the job.

When you feel the students are comfortable with some of the terminology and aspects of the system, explain the project. Have packets with the task, job descriptions, and applications ready for each team of students. Before passing out the packets stress that the students will be scored on their ability to work as a team, big buddy with little buddy, and that cooperation is the key to landing a position successfully. Set aside time for the teams to study the packet. The older buddy should read the job descriptions to the younger buddy, explaining what their responsibilities will involve. After the students have had sufficient time to review the packets, hold a question-and-answer session with the entire group. Explain that the following day they will have the opportunity to prepare their team application. After the teams have turned in the paperwork, administer the postal exam (see answer key below), stressing that scoring well on the test will help them earn a job but that it won't be the deciding factor. The application and interview will also be considered. Also, explain that if they do not receive a job this quarter they may reapply the next quarter, as the jobs will rotate throughout the year on a quarterly basis or as they become available if someone relocates.

While applications are being processed (you need to decide if you want outside help with this—perhaps elicit parent and paraprofessional assistance to conduct interviews and screen applications—or if you would prefer to do it alone), gather the entire group again and begin the process of naming the post office and deciding on street names and ZIP codes. You may do this by either taking a variety of suggestions and voting on the favorites or sticking to a theme name such as your school mascot. For example, if your school mascot is the Bears, all names could have something to do with bears, such as Cub Alley, Paddington Place, and so on. You also need to decide on a central location for the post office: your classroom, the library, or other location the students use.

When the decision has been made as to who is receiving job assignments, have a big announcement day. Congratulate the students and set up a time to introduce them to their role and responsibilities. Inform the entire student body that the post office is ready to begin operations, and let the letter writing begin.

## POSTAL EXAM ANSWER KEY

| | | |
|---|---|---|
| 1. b | 4. b | 7. b |
| 2. a | 5. c | 8. d |
| 3. d | 6. d | 9. c |

Analysis and Reflection: "P.S. Write Back Soon" Bonding Cycle

| In Progress | Basic | Proficient | Advanced | Comments |
|---|---|---|---|---|
| **STANDARDS: The levels at which students perform the task** | | | | |
| Responsibilities of the acquired position are not met.<br><br>Buddies do not cooperate or share the responsibilities of their job. | Responsibilities of the acquired position are met with minimal standards.<br><br>Work is not fully completed.<br><br>Job is done with little care and concern for details.<br><br>Both buddies contribute, but one buddy may do more than the other.<br><br>Buddies do little planning and discussion in order to complete their assignment. | Responsibilities of the acquired position are met with quality standards.<br><br>Work is completed.<br><br>Job is done with care and concern.<br><br>Workers are on time and ready to begin their assignment.<br><br>Both buddies contribute to the job most of the time.<br><br>Buddies plan and discuss job assignments in order to complete the task. | Responsibilities of the acquired position are met with high standards.<br><br>Work is totally completed.<br><br>Extreme care and concern are evident.<br><br>Workers are punctual, ready to work, and display enthusiasm.<br><br>Workers are willing to help others and do additional task without being asked.<br><br>Both buddies share full responsibility.<br><br>Buddies are able to complete the assigned job in a completely cooperative and mannerly way. | |

**Rubric 4.4**

91

# "P.S. Write Back Soon"
# Post Office Job Descriptions

## POSTMASTER

Requires a very responsible student who regularly attends school. The postmaster's hours are 15-20 minutes in the morning and 15-20 minutes in the afternoon.

1. Supervises all employees and fills in for absent employees
2. Helps train new employees
3. Possesses leadership and organizational skills, exceptional verbal skills, knowledge of all jobs, and is able to make decisions and guide other employees to work as a team

## COLLECTION CARRIERS

Responsible for picking up collection bag from postal site. Travel to each collection box located in the school, take out all mail in collection box, and return all mail to the mail handler at the postal site.

1. Able to manage behavior in the hallways
2. Report to job on time
3. Able to open collection box, remove mail, and close box

## MAIL HANDLERS

### Facer

Accepts collected mail from collection carrier. Places all mail in postal tray with address facing the front and the stamp in upper right-hand corner of envelope.

1. Able to recognize correct addressing standards
2. Has good visual discrimination skills and organizational skills

### Canceler

Cancels all stamps with postal stamp and date stamp. Makes sure that DATE ON DATE STAMP IS CHANGED EVERY DAY. Places mail back into tray and gives tray to sorters. Holds out any mail not correctly addressed and gives to Nixie Clerk.

1. Able to handle letters and hand stamp them over the postage stamp
2. Able to do a repetitive task and work independently
3. Be attentive enough to notice if a stamp is missing

## CLERKS

### Nixie Clerk

Checks for correct addressing. If not correct, stamps envelope with "Return to Sender" stamp.

1. Able to learn correct addressing standards
2. Has good visual discrimination skills, confident verbal skills, and organizational skills

### Sorters

Sort mail by ZIP code into distribution case. Then sort mail by street name into another distribution case. Bundle mail with rubber bands by streets (classrooms) for carriers.

1. Must have organizational skills
2. Know complete addressing system
3. Needs to have good eye-to-hand coordination
4. Able to work well with a team and perform with high accuracy

### Letter Carriers

Pick up the mail from the postal site and place bundles in the postal bag. Mail is then delivered to the correct classroom and placed in the mailbox that is located either outside or inside the room.

1. Able to review bundles for accuracy
2. Have knowledge of correct addressing
3. Have good organizational skills
4. Know school building and delivery route
5. Able to manage behavior in halls

# "P.S. Write Back Soon" Postal Job Application

_____ELEMENTARY SCHOOL

LAST NAME _____FIRST NAME_____

ADDRESS_____

CITY_____STATE_____ZIP CODE_____

BIRTHDATE_____          GRADE_____TEACHER_____

Position applying for:

A. Postmaster_____ B. Facer _____ C. Nixie Clerk _____D. Carrier _____E. Sorter _____

F. Collection Carrier _____ G. Canceler _____

Reference:

Teacher's Signature _____

**********************************************************************************************

## OFFICE USE ONLY

Exam score:

Interview date:

Hired: Yes                    No                    Quarter

Position Assigned:

**Figure 4.2**

# "P.S. Write Back Soon" Postal Exam

(Instructor: Substitute local city, state, and ZIP codes as necessary.)

1. Circle the correct written answer.

   a. MRS SARA WILLIAMS    c. ms sara Williams
   b. Mrs. Sara Williams      d. mrs. sara williams

2. Circle the correct written answer.

   a. Mr. Mike Johnson    c. MR MIKE JOHNSON
   b. Mr. mike johnson    d. Mr. mike Johnson

3. Circle the correct way to complete this address:

   Mrs. Sara Williams
   1000 Canoe Creek

   a. Colorado Springs Colorado 80906
   b. Colorado Springs Colorado, 80906
   c. colorodo springs, colorado 80906
   d. Colorado Springs, CO 80906

4. Circle the correct way to complete this address:

   Mr. Tim Jones
   810 Rattlesnake Way

   a. Boulder, co, 80302    c. Boulder, co, 80302
   b. Boulder, CO 80302     d. None is correct

5. Circle the set of numbers that is in the correct order from smallest to largest.

   a. 875, 870, 865    c. 985, 990, 995
   b. 995, 990, 985    d. 875, 865, 870

6. Circle the list that places the numbers in order from smallest to largest.

    a. 2504, 2500, 2508        c. 2508, 2504, 2500

    b. 2508, 2500, 2504        d. 2500, 2504, 2508

7. Which is the correct spelling?

    a. stret        c. streat

    b. street        d. sreet

8. Which is the correct spelling?

    a. colorado        c. colrado

    b. Colorodo        d. Colorado

9. Which address has the information correctly arranged?

    a. MRS. PAINTER        c. Steve Smith
       Denver, CO 81222           2616 Beaver Path
       1000 BIG CHIEF LANE      Boulder, CO 80302

    b. 550 WAMPUM WAY      d. Colorado Springs, Co
       SUE SMITH               CARLOS COOPER
       Pueblo, co, 81004          1805 ARROWHEAD

# "P.S. Write Back Soon" Postal Terms

(Suitable for K-6 and may be divided as you see fit)

## KINDERGARTEN

Address—The location where mail is to be delivered

Bundle—Several pieces of mail tied/bundled together

Delivery—Bringing the mail from the post office to the customer

Envelope—A paper folder in which a letter is mailed

Letter carrier—Mail delivery person

Mail handler—Any person who loads, unloads, or has any other job working with the mail

Mailbag/pouch—A sack in which envelopes and letters are carried

Mailbox—The mail receptacle in which the carrier leaves a customer's mail

Postage stamp—A piece of paper issued by the Postal Service and glued to the upper right-hand corner of an envelope. A stamp is the cost for processing and delivering a letter.

Workroom—The area of the post office where mail is handled

## OTHER GRADES

Bale—Large bundle of letters

Balloon—Huge pouch of mail

Brief—Formal action taken for mishandling of mail

Canceler—The person who cancels all of the stamps so they cannot be used again

Case—A piece of furniture with letter-size boxes used for sorting letters

Collector—The carrier whose duty it is to collect the mail from the street and building boxes and bring it to the post office

Dead letter—A letter dropped in the mail that is undeliverable and cannot be returned to the sender because of no return address

Faced mail—Mail arranged with the addresses and stamps all facing the same way

Facer—The person who faces the envelopes all the same way

First-class mail—Letters, postcards, and all matter partially or completely in writing

Head-out—Starting point of mail run

Hitting mail—Operation of postmarking

Indicia—An imprinted designation used on envelopes to promote community projects (the USPS indicia reads "Wee Deliver STAMP OUT ILLITERACY")

Leave—An authorized absence from your job that you must make the Postmaster aware of

Mail count—Amount of mail sorted or handled

Misthrown mail—Mail put into the wrong slots

Nixie clerks—Workers who stamp undeliverable mail "Return to Sender" when it has an insufficient address

Nixie mail—Mail that is addressed incorrectly or hard to deliver

Outgoing mail—Mail sent from one town to be delivered to another town

Philately—The collection and study of postage stamps for fun and profit

Piece—One article of mail, such as an envelope or package

Postage due—Mail on which not enough postage was paid; the amount is due when the letter is delivered

Postmark—The imprinting on the front of the letter that must be over the stamp so it cannot be used again

Postmaster—The supervisor of all mailroom workers

Second-class mail—All newspapers, magazines, and other periodicals

Shift—An employee's assigned work schedule

Slugs—Mail that is too large to be distributed in a case

Sorter—The person who sorts the mail by town and puts it in the sorting bin

Sorting machines—Machines that sort the mail by size, type, and delivery locations

Stuck—Having more mail than can be completed prior to being distributed

Tap—Collect mail from deposit box

Third-class mail—Usually advertisements, pamphlets, and merchandise weighing less than 16 ounces

Throwbacks—Mail that must be returned for distribution

Working mail—Mail that must be sorted or distributed

ZIP code—a five- or nine-digit number used to identify every delivery station (ZIP stands for Zoning Improvement Plan)

---

SOURCE: Information obtained from the United States Post Office "Wee Deliver" Program.

# "P.S. Write Back Soon" Suggested Books

| | |
|---|---|
| *Dear Daddy* | Phillipe Dupasquier |
| *Anna's Secret Friend* | Yoriko Tsutsui |
| *Letters to Horseface* | F. N. Munro |
| *The Silver Pencil* | Alice Dalgliesh |
| *Millie Cooper 3B* | Charlotte Herman |
| *Kitty Cat's Diary* | Robyn Supraner |
| *Dear Dad, Love Laurie* | Susan Beth Pfeffer |
| *Dear Diary* | Carrie Randall |
| *Friends 4-Ever* | Deirdre Corey |
| *Stringbean's Trip to the Shining Sea* | Jennifer Williams Vera and Bo Williams |
| *The Jolly Postman* | Janet and Allen Allsburg |
| *Postman Pat and the Mystery Thief* | John Cunliffe |
| *Never Mail an Elephant* | Mike Thaler |

# CONNECTION

# 5

# Interdependency of All Living Things

**Interdependency of All Living Things**

People can change their surroundings by their interactions
with plant and animal life. They are caretakers of
the land, the seas, and the skies.
Children must learn their interdependence
on all living things and their responsibility
for preserving our Earth.

# Outcomes of "Interdependency of All Living Things" Connection

| | |
|---|---|
| Students will read, research, and write as they discover problems of and answers to protecting Earth.<br><br>**LITERACY** | Students interact with adults to send the message of ecology.<br><br>**PERSONAL/SOCIAL** |
| Students will use knowledge of ecology to make decisions for the future of Earth.<br><br>**PROBLEM SOLVING** | Students learn the responsibility they have for keeping the Earth safe for living creatures.<br><br>**LIFELONG LEARNING** |
| Students realize that people around the world rely on each other to preserve Earth.<br><br>**MATHEMATIC/SCIENTIFIC REASONING** | Many job opportunities will be available for those interested in saving the environment.<br><br>**EMPLOYABILITY** |
| | Students learn to see through the camera's eye. Mounting exhibits enables them to be creative artistically.<br><br>**FINE ARTS** |

**Rubric 5.1**

101

# "Interdependency" Materials Needed

- **Primary Cycle**
  Books—Pets
  Web
  Chart paper
  Crayons

- **Intermediate Cycle**
  Books—Ecology
  Paper
  Markers
  Web

- **Bonding Cycle**
  Books—Ecology
  Cameras
  Film
  Construction paper
  Paper

# "Interdependency" Primary Cycle
## *Student Task*

## TASK

You have been asking your parents to let you have a pet, but they are unsure that you will be able to take care of one. Your job is to convince them that you know enough about the pet so that you will do a good job of taking care of it. Put together a "pet care" book. In this book you should

- name the pet you want,
- tell everything you know about it,
- name all the things it might need (a bowl if it's a fish, etc.), and
- list all of the things you will need to do on a daily, weekly, and monthly basis to care for the pet.

Remember, you are trying to convince your parents that you can take care of a pet. Be creative. You will be scored not only on the content of your book but also on how you present your information.

## CRITERIA

Following directions

Content

Presentation of material

# "Interdependency" Primary Cycle
## *Teaching Suggestions*

Begin by having a discussion about pets. Read several of the many good books published about children and their pets (see list of suggested books at the end of this segment). Continue the discussion by introducing ways that the students would need to care for different pets and why pets depend on their owners for their needs. When the students have an understanding of their responsibility to their pets, introduce the concept of webbing. Use a large chart to model the web (examples follow) about the ways they need to take care of their pets (feeding, grooming, etc.) so that they will have a shared knowledge. Repeat the activity so that the steps become familiar to the students. Using the group web, model how to write a story about how to care for a pet. Use large chart paper to write the story, encouraging the students to contribute to the writing.

Extend the activity by showing the students how to graph. First, each child draws a picture of his/her pet(s) or the animal wanted as a pet. Limit the paper size given to the students so that all of the animals will fit on the graph. When the drawings are finished, categorize them on a large graph— dogs, cats, fish, mice, and so on—and invite each child to glue his/her picture to the correct category of pet. When all have placed their drawings on the graph, ask questions such as these:

- How many dogs are owned by the class? Cats? Fish?
- Which is the most common pet?
- Which is the most unusual pet?
- Which category has the least pets?
- How many more dogs than cats are there?

If a child charts a wild animal, this is an appropriate time to discuss the needs of wild animals and why people must protect them in their native environments.

When you feel the children have a good understanding of pets and the role they need to play in a pet's life, explain the task and rubric.

## Analysis and Reflection: "Interdependency" Primary Cycle

| | STANDARDS: The levels at which students perform the task | | | Comments |
|---|---|---|---|---|
| **In Progress** | **Basic** | **Proficient** | **Advanced** | |
| Final product is incomplete and does not serve the purpose for which it was developed. | Final product shows that some of the directions were followed, and the product serves the purpose for which it was developed. | Final product shows that most of the directions were followed and adhered to and the product serves the purpose for which it was developed. | Final product shows that all directions were followed and precisely adhered to and the product serves the purpose for which it was developed. | |
| Student, even with support, is unable to provide any information on the topic. | Student, with ongoing support, is able to provide some information relevant to the topic. | Student, with minimal support, is able to provide relevant information on the topic. | Student, with no support, is able to provide relevant information on the topic. | |
| Student does not do a presentation. | Presentation lacks clarity and creativity. | Student organizes material in a logical and orderly way. | Student organizes material in a highly logical and efficient way. | |
| | | Presentation is clear and interesting. | Presentation reflects knowledge, creativity, and independence and is given in a clear, enthusiastic manner. | |

**Rubric 5.2**

# Webbing—Primary Cycle

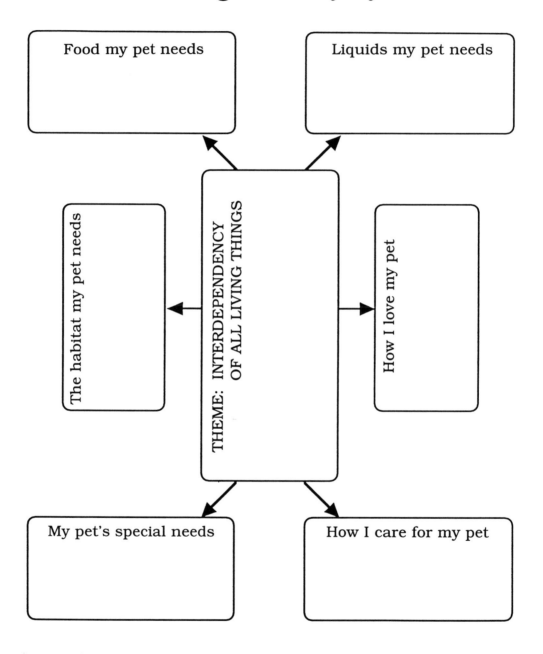

**Figure 5.1**

# Webbing—Primary Cycle

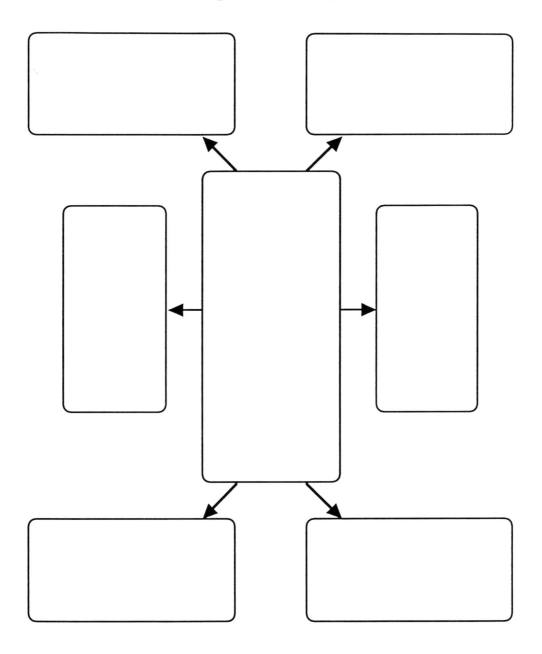

**Figure 5.2**

# "Interdependency"
# Suggested Books on Pets

| | |
|---|---|
| *Dear Zoo* | Rod Campbell |
| *Mary's Pets* | Clive Scruton |
| *Eric Carle's Animals, Animals* | Eric Carle |
| *The Kids' World Almanac of Animals and Pets* | Deborah G. Felder |
| *Animal Partners: Training Animals to Help People* | Patricia Curtis |
| *Introducing Pets* | Debra Wasserman |
| *Your First Pet and How to Take Care of It* | Carla Stevens |
| *All About Cats as Pets* | Majorie Zaum |
| *The Dog That Called the Signals* | Matt Christopher |
| *To Love a Cat* | Colleen Stanley Bare |

# "Interdependency" Intermediate Cycle
## *Student Task*

## TASK

Earth means many different things to the people who live here. For some it is the wide open spaces, the mountains, or the big city. Whatever Earth's meaning, we now know that we can no longer abuse it the way we have in the past. One way that we in America have called attention to the pollution of Earth's waters, air, and land is to celebrate Earth Day. On this day we send the message to all citizens to conserve water, dispose of waste properly, and protect the air we breathe and the land we walk on.

Your task is to create a series of ecology cards that will remind citizens of the importance of Earth Day. Each card should have a written and a visual message and represent a different area of concern. One card might mention the factories and how they are polluting our rivers and air. Another might be a call for citizens to recycle trash, reusing all that they can. You will be given the opportunity to read and research, so the ideas for your cards will be innumerable. Think about what is important to you and in what condition you want to leave the Earth for your children and grandchildren. The best cards will be sent to a card publishing company and/or a sign board company, so do your best. Each card should be written correctly, be illustrated, and send a definite message. You are expected to turn in a bibliography or list showing books and resources used for ecology information.

## CRITERIA

Research skills

Knowledge of ecology

Written cards

# "Interdependency" Intermediate Cycle
## *Teaching Suggestions*

Begin by having a discussion about ecology. Determine prior knowledge by grouping students and giving each group a large piece of paper on which to list everything it knows about the topic. After a few minutes, rotate the papers, asking one group to read the thoughts of the other group and to add any information that is not on the chart. Continue this process until all groups have read and added to each chart.

Read a simple introductory book about ecology to the class and encourage students to begin reading and researching on their own. Model how to web the information they find. (Both specific and blank outlines follow.) Stress the responsibility of people to their surroundings.

At this point, students should have an understanding of pollution of the air, water, and land. They should be aware of both plants and animals that have become extinct because of people's misuse of them. Give students a web to complete as they research. They can use the generic web or create one of their own.

When the research, reading, and webbing have been completed, model the making of the Earth Day card. If you have made one or can find a premade card, show it to the students as a standard for excellence. Hand out the rubric so that students can refer to it as they create their cards. Post one copy of the assessment on the board for all to see while they work. Be aware that a few always get lost during the project.

Give students the materials they need to complete their ecology cards. Each card should include a written message informing the reader how he/she is responsible for the Earth and what can be done for future generations. Illustrations should be coordinated with the text of the card.

Be sure to emphasize the importance of writing for an audience. This means that students will need to peer edit to remove all errors in spelling, punctuation, and grammar. Constantly refer the students back to the rubric and the standard of excellence presented in the models.

When card sets are completed, send copies of them to card companies. They might accept some of the cards or be interested in developing a new category for cards that celebrate Earth Day. Local sign board agencies might be willing to donate space on unrented billboards to promote the students' messages. It's good PR for them and they can deduct the cost of renting the billboard.

# Analysis and Reflection: "Interdependency" Intermediate Cycle

## STANDARDS: The levels at which students perform the task

| In Progress | Basic | Proficient | Advanced | Comments |
|---|---|---|---|---|
| Student uses one data source. Sources are not complete or are left out. Most of the writing appears to be word-for-word copying of the information from the source. Web is incomplete and/or incorrect. Purpose of the cards is not achieved. Cards are unacceptable. Errors in spelling, punctuation, and grammar interfere with the meaning. Pictures, drawings, or graphs have no importance to understanding ecology. | Student uses a minimum of two data sources. Sources are identified. Much of the writing is in the student's language, but there may be some word-for-word copying of information from sources. Web has details, shows some new knowledge of ecology, and is complete for the most part. Purpose of the cards is achieved. Cards are acceptable. There are some errors in spelling, punctuation, and grammar, but they do not interfere with the meaning. Pictures, drawings, or charts have some importance to ecology. | Student uses a minimum of three data sources. Sources are mostly cited correctly. There is some evidence that these sources guide the writing. Web is detailed, correct, and shows new knowledge about ecology. Purpose of the cards is evident. Cards are attractive. Cards have few errors in spelling, punctuation, and grammar. Pictures, drawings, or graphs add to the understanding of ecology. | Student uses a minimum of four data sources. Sources are cited appropriately. There is clear evidence that these sources guide the writing. Web is detailed, complete, correct, and shows new information about ecology. Purpose of the cards is totally achieved. Cards are appealing in every way. There is evidence of editing, with minimal or no errors in spelling, punctuation, and grammar. Pictures, drawings, or graphs highlight the importance of ecology. | |

**Rubric 5.3**

111

# Webbing —Intermediate Cycle

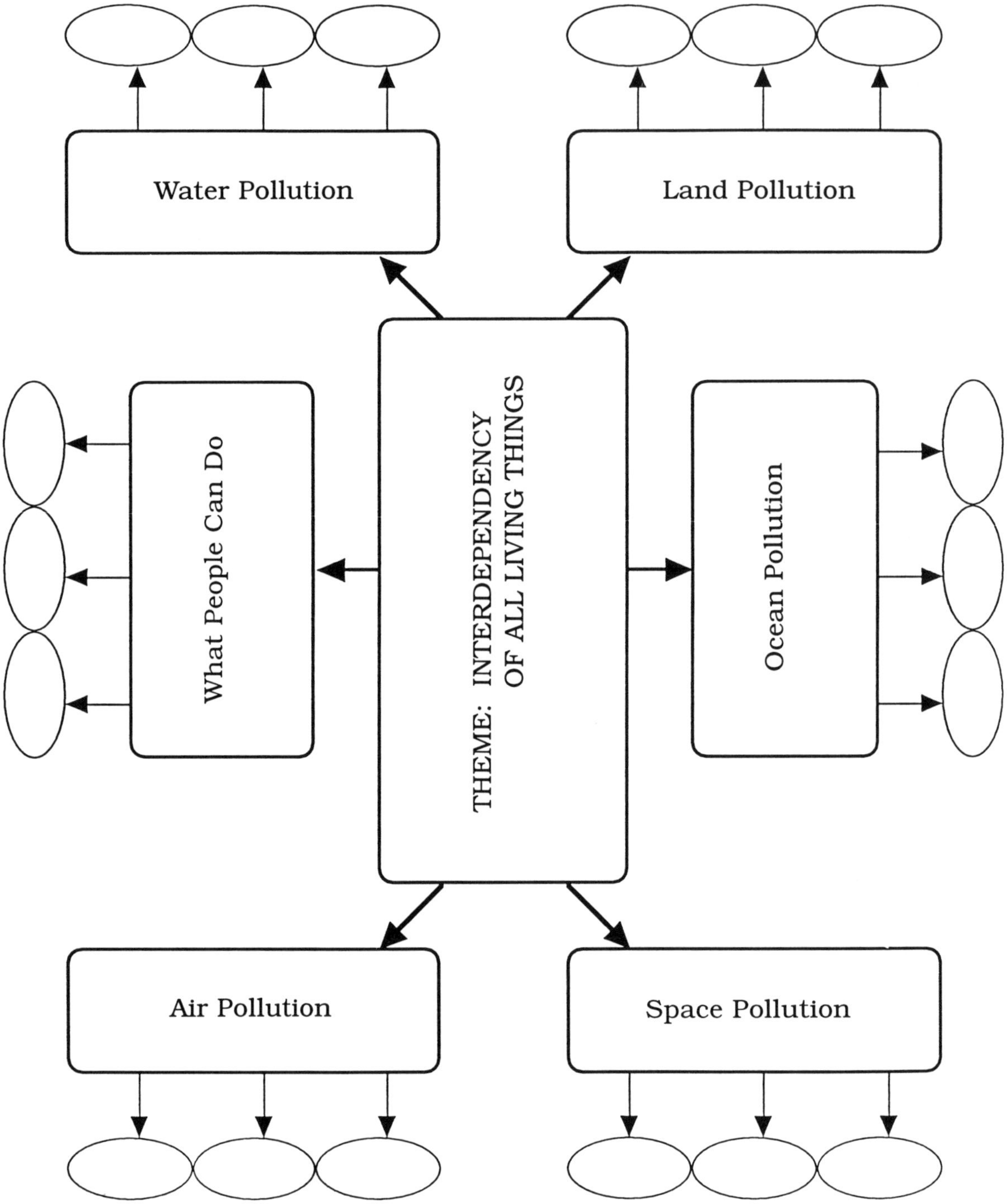

Water Pollution

Land Pollution

What People Can Do

THEME: INTERDEPENDENCY OF ALL LIVING THINGS

Ocean Pollution

Air Pollution

Space Pollution

**Figure 5.3**

# Webbing—Intermediate Cycle

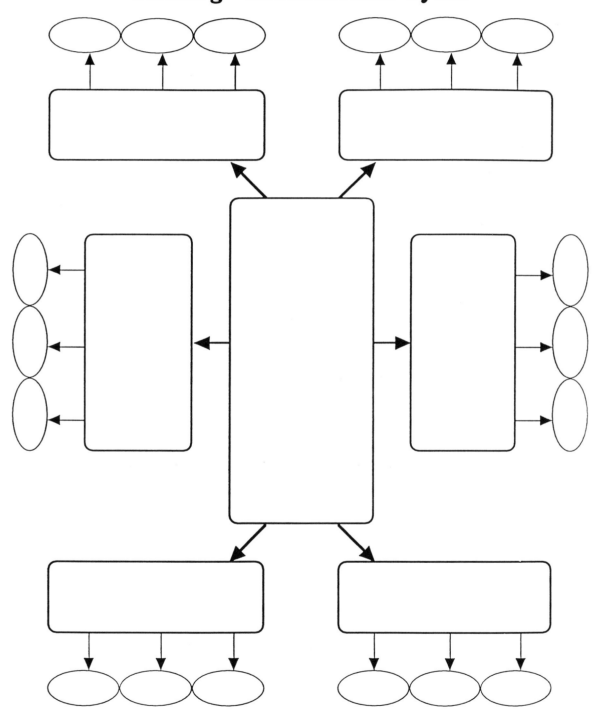

**Figure 5.4**

# "Interdependency" Bonding Cycle
## *Student Task*

### TASK

A tragic event happened over 100 years ago. Americans from the North and the South fought against each other for the first time. This bitter battle would be lost to us today if it weren't for men like the photographer Matthew Brady who followed the camps of the soldiers.

Today we are fighting a war with our environment. Our land, water, and air are becoming unfit for human use. The task for you and your buddy is to become the Matthew Brady of the 20th century by creating a photo display of the pollution and waste that you see around you.

You need to begin with an in-depth study of ecology, the study of the relationship of living organisms and their environments. Following your study, photograph examples of pollution or waste that you find in your school or your community. When your photos are developed, study them, classify them, date them, and state where they were taken. Include a brief description of the impact that you think each photo will have.

Mount your pictures for the open house that will bring in family and friends to share your concerns.

### CRITERIA

Photo display
Preparation sheets

# "Interdependency" Bonding Cycle
## *Teaching Suggestions*

This activity is one that buddy pairs will love, but it does require a camera and film. Most parents will be willing to donate film, and students can usually obtain an inexpensive camera from family or friends. If students cannot get these items, they can draw pictures of the ecology problems they find and mount these just as they would photographs.

If it is possible, find some of the Civil War photos taken by Matthew Brady. Discuss the importance of the pictures to people who have only read about the war. Stress that the pictures have brought the actual event to our mind's eye and remind us all of the horrors of that war. Explain that the buddies will have the same opportunity to preserve the battle to save Earth. They will be able to take photos of places that people need to take better care of and areas where people have made the effort to clean up the air, water, or land.

Because the older buddies will have already studied some ecology, they can use this background to begin thinking of their pictorial presentations. It will be up to the big buddy to share this information and to help the little buddy read for new information.

It is important to involve the parents of both groups in this activity as most of the pictures will likely be taken away from the school environment. We suggest that you schedule an evening on which you invite the parents to school, explain the activity, and ask for their support. You will be surprised by the positive response you receive. Parents are usually quite willing to drive buddy pairs around the community to find places where there is waste and reclamation that they would want to photograph for their display. If, for some reason, parents are not able to help, then take the buddy pairs on a walking tour through the community so they can take photos of what they find. Results could be presented at local community centers, churches, libraries, and so on. One word of warning: The students must think about the big picture and not the neighbor's trash that has fallen on the ground. You don't want to ruin any relationships among friends of education!

After their photographs have been developed, the students complete the Photo Plan, mount their photos, and write an explanation on how each picture will affect future people who will live on the Earth we leave them.

Finally, make a display of the photos and explanations and invite parents to view the thoughts of their children. Call local banks and office buildings to see if the display can be set up for public viewing.

# Analysis and Reflection: "Interdependency" Bonding Cycle

## STANDARDS: The levels at which students perform the task

| In Progress | Basic | Proficient | Advanced | Comments |
|---|---|---|---|---|
| Purpose of the photo display is not achieved. | Purpose of the photo display is achieved. | Purpose of the photo display is evident. | Purpose of the photo display is totally achieved. | |
| Planning sheets are not used, and picture explanations are incomplete and/or incorrect. | Planning sheets are partially used so that picture explanations have some detail and are mostly correct. | Planning sheets are used so that picture explanations are complete and correct. | Planning sheets are used so that picture explanations are detailed, complete, and correct. | |
| Pictures and explanations are difficult to follow and lack clarity. | Pictures and explanations are understandable. | Pictures and explanations are generally clear, logical, and in sequential order. | Pictures and explanations are very clear, logical, and in sequential order. | |
| Mounted pictures are unacceptable. | Mounted pictures are acceptable. | Mounted pictures are attractive. | Mounted pictures are appealing in every way. | |
| Accuracy of information is questionable. | There is some evidence of accuracy. | Accuracy of information is obvious. | Accuracy of information is total. | |
| Errors in spelling, punctuation, and grammar interfere with the meaning. | Errors in spelling, punctuation, and grammar do not interfere with the meaning. | There are few errors in spelling, punctuation, and grammar. | There is evidence of editing, with minimal or no errors in spelling, punctuation, and grammar. | |

**Rubric 5.4**

*Clip photo here*

# "Interdependency" Photo Plan

This photo was taken by _____

Subject of photograph: _____

Date of photograph: _____

Site of photograph: _____

We have decided to include the photograph in our show because

_____

_____

_____

We have decided NOT to include the photograph in our show because

_____

_____

_____

We have decided to write an editorial to the paper because

_____

_____

_____

We have decided NOT to write an editorial to the paper because

_____

_____

_____

**Figure 5.5**

# "Interdependency"
# Suggested Books on Ecology

| | |
|---|---|
| *Nature's Great Balancing Act: In Your Own Backyard* | E. Jaediker Norsgaard |
| *The Seashore Book* | Charlotte Zolotow |
| *Little Elephant's Walk* | Adrienne Kennaway |
| *Blast Off to Earth! A Look at Geography* | Loreen Leedy |
| *Going Green: A Kid's Handbook to Saving the Planet* | John Elkington, Julia Hailes, Douglas Hill, and Joe Makower |
| *The Old Ladies Who Liked Cats* | Carol Green |
| *The World That Jack Built* | Ruth Brown |
| *Our Earth: A Multitude of Creatures* | Peter Roop and Connie Roop |
| *The Salamander Room* | Anne Mazer |
| *The Day the Lifting Bridge Stuck* | Robert Yagelski |
| *A River Ran Wild* | Lynne Cherry |
| *Rain Drops Splash* | Alvin Tressett |
| *River Keeper* | George Ancona |
| *Save the Earth: An Action Handbook for Kids* | Betty Miles |

# CONNECTION

# 6

# Creations

---

**Creations**

People's ability to create, invent, and produce
is the quality that sets them apart from
all other living creatures on Earth.
Whether they create original works of art,
discover new laws of nature,
or invent something for their own use,
people's ability to think makes them unequaled.
Young people can be challenged to reach the same heights
of those who have gone before them.
All they need is the opportunity.

# Outcomes of "Creations" Connection

| | | |
|---|---|---|
| Students will read about advertising and inventions. They will write and present orally. | Students will plan and work together for a purpose of communicating to others. | Understanding the purpose of advertising and the progress of invention will give students life-long skills. |
| **LITERACY** | **PERSONAL/SOCIAL** | **LIFELONG LEARNING** |
| Students will have to make decisions on advertising methods and in creating new inventions. | | Students will use their creative abilities as they make ads to attract the attention of others. |
| **PROBLEM SOLVING** | | **FINE ARTS** |
| Students will understand the concepts of personal and environmental interdependence in the ads they create. | Many job opportunities can be found in advertising and the science fields. | In studying inventions and in creating original inventions, students will be introduced to the technological world. |
| **MATHEMATIC/SCIENTIFIC REASONING** | **EMPLOYABILITY** | **TECHNOLOGICAL LITERACY** |

**Rubric 6.1**

# "Creations" Materials Needed

- **Primary Cycle**
  Craft sticks
  Clay
  Boxes
  Tubes
  Assorted materials
      Balances
      Magnets
      Old radios
      Old telephones
  Tools
      Hammers
      Balances
      Screwdrivers
      Wood
      Nails
      Screws
      Pliers

- **Intermediate Cycle**
  Books—Advertising
  Chart paper
  Tag board
  Markers
  Magazines

- **Bonding Cycle**
  Books—Inventions and Inventors
  Milk cartons
  Tubes
  Glue
  Scissors
  Aluminum foil
  Various boxes
  Wood
  Nails
  Craft sticks
  Chart paper
  Tag board
  Markers

# "Creations" Primary Cycle
## *Student Task*

## TASK

A new park is going to be constructed in your neighborhood. The company in charge of building this park is asking for your input. They want to know what kind of equipment you would like to have and what type of structures you would enjoy the most. They are asking you to design the play equipment for the new park, make a model of it, and submit it to their planning board within two weeks. They want as many details as possible to help them know exactly what you would like the park to look like.

You may use craft sticks, clay, or any other medium you think would work best. Your design will be judged on neatness, creativity, and evidence of an organizational plan.

## CRITERIA

Neatness

Creativity

Organization

# "Creations" Primary Cycle
## *Teaching Suggestions*

Young people love to see how things move, work, operate, and "go." Many times they can be found taking apart and putting back together anything they can get their hands on. To encourage this curiosity, allow time for students to explore many different kinds of simple machines, balances, magnets, old radios, old telephones, and so forth. Provide them with hammers, wood, nails, screwdrivers, pliers, and other tools that would lend themselves to fixing, taking apart, and putting back together. This open exploration should be completely student directed. They can discover so much if they are not stifled in any way. Do provide, however, books and materials that also show pictures of machines, building things, and simple projects that can be done with craft sticks or other such materials. This involvement with different materials will not only help when they are working on their own task but also give them the needed exposure to making a "creation" when working with their buddy.

After you feel the students have had enough time to explore, tinker, and work with the materials, explain the task and rubric. Explain that they may do the project at home, using materials they can find around the house, or that you will give them sufficient time to complete the project at school. (This is something you need to decide before assigning the task.)

After all projects have been completed, encourage the students to select one park design they think best represents quality work and to prepare a rationale as to why this park design should be built in their neighborhood. Their ideas can then be presented to the neighborhood association, school board, or community civic groups for construction considerations.

# Analysis and Reflection: "Creations" Primary Cycle

## STANDARDS: The levels at which students perform the task

| In Progress | Basic | Proficient | Advanced | Comments |
|---|---|---|---|---|
| Student cannot stay focused on project. | Student can focus on project for short periods of time. | Student stays focused on project for lengthy periods of time. | Student can stay focused while working and is looking for ways to improve project when not working. | |
| Student gets frustrated very easily. | Student gets frustrated if plan does not work. | Student shows little or no frustration and asks for help when needed. | Student needs no help and shows confidence. | |
| Project is incomplete. | Project is somewhat complete but lacks neatness and creativity. | Project is complete and neat, with some creativity evident. | Project is complete, extremely neat, and original in thought and design. | |
| Project is not neat. | | | | |
| No organizational plan is evident. | Organizational plan is weak. | Organizational plan is evident. | Organizational plan is evident and adds to the overall effect. | |

**Rubric 6.2**

# "Creations" Intermediate Cycle
## *Student Task*

## TASK

Most advertising campaigns urge people to buy goods or services. However, there are advertising campaigns that urge people to accept a point of view.

Your task is to create an advertising campaign to persuade readers to support something you feel strongly about. How do you feel about crime, and how do you think we can prevent it? How can taking care of the air affect the reader? How can banning smoking help the non-smoker?

Decide on an issue that you wish to make a statement on and research the topic to collect data that will both support and counter your position. Once your cause is determined, study the different ways of advertising so that you can create a portfolio of different ideas. Select a minimum of five different forms of advertising that you will use to get your point across to the public. Design an ad for each advertising form you have chosen.

Remember, the best way to influence people is to create ads that appeal to their self-interest, arouse their curiosity, and offer them news or information.

Also, be sure that your ad campaign attracts attention, arouses interest, creates desire, ensures belief, and impels action.

## CRITERIA

Knowledge of topic

Knowledge of advertising techniques

Visual and written advertisements

# "Creations" Intermediate Cycle
## *Teaching Suggestions*

Begin this study by showing students advertisements. Bring examples from newspapers, magazines, catalogs, or direct mailings. Discuss what these advertisements do for the companies that send them out or produce them and their value to the businesses. Lead the discussion to the fact that there are other types of advertisements that try to persuade people to accept certain points of view. Try to find examples of these types of ads as they will help the students better understand this area of advertising.

Hand out the rubric and explain that the students are going to create five different ads that make a statement. You might want to involve the students in a group discussion and list some of the ideas they want to support. Encourage originality. Those who feel less creative can select from the list that you have posted in the room for all to see. Explain to the students that they will need to study their topic, brainstorm some ideas for the ads, and come to a decision about the kinds of advertisements they would like to make. These could include a newspaper ad, a magazine ad, a radio ad, a television ad (which could be videotaped), a poster ad for a community business, a catalog ad, or a letter mailed to citizens. Encourage the students to spend some time studying advertisements—what makes them effective, what makes them eye appealing, and what types are remembered (jingles, two-line rhymes, etc.). Students can study magazines, newspapers, mail ads, and television ads and listen to the radio to find examples. Set aside time for discussion and planning before giving them the materials to make their ads. Then, turn them loose. You will be surprised by the results, and the students will really enjoy the activity.

# Analysis and Reflection: "Creations" Intermediate Cycle

## STANDARDS: The levels at which students perform the task

| In Progress | Basic | Proficient | Advanced | Comments |
|---|---|---|---|---|
| One or no points support the issue/cause. Ads do not fulfill the criteria for effective advertising. One or no medium is used to create the portfolio. Visual ads are ineffective. Errors in spelling, grammar, and punctuation interfere with the meaning. Student is unable to explain the portfolio. Overall, the ad campaign is ineffective. Student is unable to stay focused while working on the task. | A few major points of the issue/cause are presented. Ads meet at least three of the criteria for good advertising. At least three different mediums are used to create the portfolio. Visual ads are acceptable. Errors in spelling, grammar, or punctuation do not interfere with the meaning. Student is able to explain the issue/cause and portfolio. Student stays focused and on task much of the time. Overall, the ad campaign is understandable. | Most of the major points of the issue/cause are presented. Ads meet at least four of the criteria for good advertising. At least four different mediums are used to create the portfolio. Visual ads are attractive. There is some evidence of editing, and errors do not interfere with the meaning. Reader feels that the point is made. Student explains the cause/issue in detail. Student is involved in the project during working periods. The points of the ad campaign are related, and the overall portfolio is effective. | All major points of the issue/cause are presented. Ads meet the five criteria for outstanding advertisements. Five or more ads in different mediums are presented in the portfolio. Visual ads are attractive in every way. There is evidence of editing, with few or no errors in spelling, grammar, or punctuation. Readers are totally influenced by the ad campaign. Student presents the issue/cause in a winning way. Student is totally involved in the project the entire working time. The overall effect is out-standing. | |

**Rubric 6.3**

127

# "Creations" Advertisement Planning

The topic/cause that I will promote to the public is

_____

_____

_____

The points that I will emphasize are

_____

_____

_____

The types of advertisement that I will promote are

_____

_____

_____

My plans are to do the following:

_____

_____

_____

The art/visual work that I will do is

_____

_____

_____

# "Creations" Bonding Cycle
## *Student Task*

## TASK

By definition, an invention is putting ideas and materials together to make something that did not exist before. People's curiosity and their desire to satisfy basic needs for survival result in creating new ideas. They then use these ideas along with available materials to create inventions.

Today we use many inventions that we take for granted. We forget that they once only existed in the minds of others. Ask your grandmothers if many years ago they used a little box to bake a potato in minutes instead of hours.

The task for you and your buddy is to invent something, build a prototype of it, and create an advertising campaign that will convince a manufacturer to believe in your idea enough to produce it for you.

First, you need to read about inventions and inventors so that you will have a common background. Then, interview family and friends to determine inventions that they feel would make life easier or more enjoyable. For instance, if mowing the lawn is a chore your brother hates, invent an electronic machine to do it for him. Your invention can be as complicated as the electronic lawn mower or as simple as a way to keep your glasses from becoming soiled. Use your imagination and the Interview Questionnaire to help you.

As you gather information, decide on the project that you will design. Research what is known about the idea and design your invention on paper. From your plans, begin to construct your idea together. Use any materials that you and your buddy can find and that are safe.

When your prototype is complete, create an advertising campaign to convince a manufacturer that your idea is feasible and will bring profit to the company if it decides to manufacture it.

Finally, send your plans, your advertising campaign, and a letter of explanation to any companies that you feel might be responsive to your invention.

## CRITERIA

Research for ideas and
  background information

Written plans

Prototype

Advertising campaign

Letters

# "Creations" Bonding Cycle
## *Teaching Suggestions*

Begin this activity by talking about inventions. Ask the buddy pairs to give examples of inventions and what they do for us. List these and point out different inventions around the classroom. Stress what the inventions do for us. Ask the students what they would do without the pencil sharpener, for instance, or even the pencil. They will enjoy this discussion, which provides a good background for the bonding activity.

By definition, an invention is a device or process originated after study and experiment. Explain that the students are going to have the opportunity to be inventors and create something that will benefit everyone. Hand out the rubric and go over it with the buddies. Encourage the buddy pairs to interview their families, especially older relatives such as grandparents. The Interview Questionnaire will help the pairs decide on their own inventions. When these interviews are brought back, encourage students to share their findings about inventions and how they have changed our lives and what people would like to have invented to help their lives now.

Suggest that the buddies read about the most famous inventions and inventors. This reading will also help them decide what they want to create.

Once they have decided on an invention, the buddies should read about the area they want to develop. They will discover what has already been created and how they can expand on what is already known. Then ask the students to bring in the materials they will need to make a prototype of their invention.

Once the prototype is done, the students need to create an advertising campaign. The older buddies will have already learned about advertising and so will be able to help the little buddies participate. This is the fun part, and students will love presenting their inventions and ads to the rest of the class.

# Analysis and Reflection: "Creations" Bonding Cycle

## STANDARDS: The levels at which students perform the task

| In Progress | Basic | Proficient | Advanced | Comments |
|---|---|---|---|---|
| Purpose of the project is not achieved. Project shows no evidence of research for new knowledge. Project is incomplete and/or incorrect. Errors in spelling, grammar, and punctuation greatly interfere with the meaning. There is no evidence of editing the written work. Prototype is constructed without plans. Letters do not follow correct business letter form. No letters are sent to companies. Students are not able to stay focused on the project and argue with each other. | Purpose of the project is somewhat achieved. Information presented in the portfolio shows minimal research for new information. Ad campaign has details and is generally complete. Written plans have a main idea but few details to support it. Some errors in spelling, grammar, and punctuation occasionally interfere with the meaning. There is some evidence of editing the written work. Prototype follows plans and is generally neat. Letters follow business letter form. At least one letter is sent to a company. Students are able to focus on the project without disagreement, but one buddy might do the majority of the task. | Purpose of the project is evident. Information in the portfolio shows that research was completed. Ad campaign is detailed, complete, and correct. Written plans have a main idea and supporting explanations. Errors in spelling, grammar, and punctuation do not interfere with the meaning. Prototype follows plans and is constructed neatly. Letters follow correct business letter form. At least two letters are sent to companies. Students are mostly focused on the task, with both contributing ideas and work. Purpose of the project is totally achieved. | Information presented in the portfolio shows evidence of thorough research for new knowledge. Ad campaign is well detailed, complete, and correct. Written plans are well defined with many explanations and details. There are minimal or no errors in spelling, grammar, and punctuation. There is strong evidence of editing the written work. Prototype follows plans and is well constructed in every aspect. Letters follow correct business letter form. At least three letters are sent to companies. Students are totally involved in the project and share both work and ideas. | |

**Rubric 6.4**

131

# "Creations" Interview Questionnaire

What inventions do you appreciate the most?

_____

_____

What inventions make your work easier?

_____

_____

What do you feel are the greatest inventions of the 20th century?

_____

_____

Would you like someone to create an invention that would do your chores for you? What chores?

_____

_____

Do you have any ideas for new inventions?

_____

_____

Are there products that you would like to have that do not now exist?

_____

_____

Why are certain products and inventions so important to the people who use them? Are these characteristics important in creating your own invention?

_____

_____

# "Creations" Invention Plans

We plan to invent

_____

_____

_____

We feel our invention is important because

_____

_____

_____

Materials we will need to draw our plans are

_____

_____

_____

Materials we will need to build our prototype are

_____

_____

_____

The way we plan to conduct our advertising campaign is by

_____

_____

_____

Manufacturers and companies that we will send our ideas to are

_____

_____

_____

## AGENCIES THAT HELP WITH INVENTIONS

Several government agencies and private organizations offer publications and assistance to independent inventors. Here are a few of them:

- U.S. Patent and Trademark Office, 1-703-557-4636
- U.S. Business Administration, 1-800-827-5722
- U.S. Federal Trade Commission, 1-202-326-2502
- National Congress of Inventor Organizations, 1-800-753-0888
- United Inventors Association of the United States of America (UIA-USA), P.O. Box 50305, St. Louis, MO 63105. Send a stamped, self-addressed envelope.

# "Creations" Suggested Books

| | |
|---|---|
| *The Great American Idea Book* | Bob Coleman |
| *The Inventor Through History* | Peter Lafferty |
| *Women Inventors and Their Discoveries* | Ethlie Ann Var |
| *Invention: The Care and Feeding of Ideas* | Norbert Wiener |
| *Eureka! It's a Telephone* | Jeanne Bendick |
| *Eureka! It's a Television* | Jeanne Bendick |
| *Eureka! It's an Automobile* | Jeanne Bendick |
| *Marketing Your Invention* | Thomas Mosley |
| *I Didn't Know That! About How Things Work* | Anthony Tallarico |
| *Inventors and Inventions* | Michael Jeffries |
| *Forks, Phonographs and Hot Air Balloons* | Robert Weber |
| *Inventions That Affect Our Lives* | Software; Orange Cherry, $39.00 |

# CONNECTION

# 7

# Experiencing Art

---

**Art**

Art is the medium by which people are able to unite
their creative imagination with their ingenuity and skills
to create a thing of beauty.
In every soul there is an appreciation of
something aesthetic, something beyond
the routine and ordinary, something that raises
us above ourselves.
Young people, unencumbered by inhibition,
deserve the chance to reach these heights.

# Outcomes of "Experiencing Art" Connection

| | | |
|---|---|---|
| Students will have the opportunity to study the creative work of artists from past and present. | Students will be writing, reading, and discussing art. They will learn what others value. | Students will study works of art and decide what is beauty to them. |
| **FINE ARTS** | **LITERACY** | **PROBLEM SOLVING** |
| Many students are able to express themselves through their artistic abilities. Many jobs need these skills. | The arts give students the opportunity to reach within and discover beauty. | Buddies will discuss characteristics of art and share ideas of what is beautiful. |
| **EMPLOYABILITY** | **LIFELONG LEARNING** | **PERSONAL/SOCIAL** |

**Rubric 7.1**

# "Experiencing Art" Materials Needed

- **Primary Cycle**

  Books—Great works of art

  Pictures

  Paintings

- **Intermediate Cycle**

  Books—Artists

  Paper for murals

  Markers

- **Bonding Cycle**

  Books—Artworks, architecture, fine art

  Brochures of art

  Paper

  Binding materials

  Markers

# "Experiencing Art" Primary Cycle
## *Student Task*

**TASK**

Art is all around us. Everywhere we look we see color, size, shape, and beauty. We have a history of art and artists who have tried to capture this beauty for us in their own ways. You have been exposed to many different art forms and artists and you have been discussing how you interpret their work. You and a partner will have the opportunity to do this on your own with a new art print.

Here is your job. Working with your partner, choose a picture from those available. Look at it, talk to your partner about it, and share your feelings about it. Then, fill out the Story Planning Sheet and be ready to share your story with the class.

**CRITERIA**

Story

# "Experiencing Art" Primary Cycle
*Teaching Suggestions*

Exposure to various types of art and artists introduces the students to a number of skills. Using art as the focus, discuss attributes such as color, size, and shape. Collect as many prints as you can to share with the students. In the discussion, talk about what colors were used, how they blend together, the differences in shades and highlights, and the mediums used, and then afford the students the opportunity to add what they see and how they interpret the print. Continue the discussion with other attributes of the picture until the children feel comfortable talking about what they see and how it makes them feel. This is a good time to use the five senses to describe the picture. How might it smell if you were in the setting? What might you be touching? What would it sound like if you were in the middle of the crowd?

To take this activity one step further and incorporate higher-level thinking skills into this model, teach the students how to use the picture to make up a story. This will involve a lot of inferring on their part, but with some guidance it can be accomplished. Use of the 5 Ws helps the students begin thinking and using what they see to make up a story. Start out by asking them to name the characters (the people in the picture) and describe what they might be like (nice, funny, etc.). Then go on to the setting—where is it? Where might it be leading? Where were they before they got to where they are? Continue in this fashion until you feel the students have shared enough and have enough information that they will be able to tell a story about the picture. Because the task is similar to this activity, work with the students until they feel confident and you feel they can handle the task on their own. Explain the task and rubric and encourage them to begin working.

Analysis and Reflection: "Experiencing Art" Primary Cycle

| | STANDARDS: The levels at which students perform the task | | | |
|---|---|---|---|---|
| **In Progress** | **Basic** | **Proficient** | **Advanced** | **Comments** |
| Story does not include characters, setting, or events. | Story includes basics about characters, setting, and events. | Story includes many details about characters, setting, and events. | Story includes extensive details about characters, setting, and events. | |
| No other ideas that add interest are present. | Other ideas are present and make story more interesting. | Many ideas are present and make story more interesting. | Extensive ideas are present and make story interesting and enjoyable. | |
| Student may merely show print but not extend thinking. | Student shows print and makes up simple story about picture. | Student shows print, and story goes into detail. | Student shows print, and story goes along with picture. | |
| | Student uses story form. | Student uses story form. | Creativity is evident. | |
| | | | Storyteller's feelings are evident. | |
| | | | Story form is followed and own ideas are evident. | |

**Rubric 7.2**

140

# "Experiencing Art" Story Planning Sheet

Characters _____

_____

_____

_____

Setting _____

_____

_____

_____

What is happening _____

_____

_____

_____

What might happen _____

_____

_____

_____

Ideas we want to add to make the story more interesting _____

_____

_____

_____

# "Experiencing Art" Intermediate Cycle
## *Student Task*

## TASK

The support of art depends on adults who appreciate its aesthetic beauty and its importance in the lives of people. As young people you will be the next generation to support your local museums with your patronage. Your local museum is asking all school districts to ensure continued support by creating units of study that compare and contrast different artists and their styles. They have asked your classroom to do an in-depth study of 10-15 artists from long ago through today. The museum wants you to study each artist's works, note the elements of style, and study the artist's history. Your task is to create a montage that shows your findings. Your montage can be made of any pictures, drawings, or other media that help you express the artists and their styles, and what makes them outstanding and notable. Also, be prepared to present your mural in a 2- to 5-minute oral presentation.

## CRITERIA

Research skills

Content of mural

Oral presentation

# "Experiencing Art" Intermediate Cycle
## *Teaching Suggestions*

For intermediate students to fully appreciate the "Experiencing Art" task, it is important to expose them to the myriad of art forms that artists have used to express their creative talents.

Begin with an initial discussion of the meaning of art. Building on the students' understanding, help them expand their definitions to include carving, ceramics, engraving, photography, sculpture, quilting, or any other art forms they recognize as a means of expression. Bring in examples of as many of the forms as you can. If few are available, magazines provide a basis for discussion.

Once students are able to appreciate the many forms of aesthetic expression, introduce them to the varied styles of art. This can be accomplished with a visit to a local museum. If this is not possible, prints can be found in books in your local library. In fact, many of the larger museums will send prints and slide presentations to schools for viewing.

Contact local art stores, local artists, the school art teacher, older art students, parents, and anyone else who might share the arts from all countries and all periods of history. Students can write to the major organizations that sponsor art to ask for brochures.

Inundate your students with materials and experiences and then turn them loose with the task. Encourage them to read, study, draw, and express the assignment in a truly artistic, aesthetic way.

Analysis and Reflection: "Experiencing Art" Intermediate Cycle

| STANDARDS: The levels at which students perform the task | | | | |
|---|---|---|---|---|
| In Progress | Basic | Proficient | Advanced | Comments |
| Student relies totally on one resource for information, probably an encyclopedia. Student is unable to cross-reference. Student makes no effort to bring in outside resources. Mural does not achieve the task. Purpose is not achieved. Pictures and drawings are unrelated to the artists, showing no comparison or contrast. Mural is a series of pictures/drawings that are unconnected. Student reads oral presentation, and delivery is awkward. Little or no eye contact is made. | Student uses limited resources to find information. Student cannot go beyond using the artist's name to find materials. Student limits reading to resources in the class/school library but attempts to bring in outside resources. Purpose of the mural is achieved but limited in information. Art is limited to one medium. Mural shows some organization in its development. Student relies on note cards for oral presentation but reads in an interesting way. Infrequent eye contact is made. | Student uses multiple resources but relies primarily on two or three. Student uses an index and can cross-reference for further information. Purpose of the mural is achieved and is mostly complete. At least 10 artists' works are compared and contrasted. Student selects a wide range of art mediums but may not represent a variety of periods of art. Mural is attractive and shows effort in its development. Student recites most of the information and speaks in a voice that can be heard by all in the audience. Eye contact is made the majority of the time. | Student uses multiple resources, including magazines, pamphlets, and brochures to find information. Student cross-references as information is found, and one idea leads to another. Student brings information from outside resources, such as museums, letters, displays, or interviews. Purpose of mural is complete and appealing in every way. Ten to 15 artists are represented, and various works are compared and contrasted. Student selects a variety of art from different periods. Selections show thought and purpose. The mural shows imagination and effort in development. Explanation is clear, and enthusiasm is evident. There is total eye contact. | |

Rubric 7.3

# "Experiencing Art" Bonding Cycle
## *Student Task*

## TASK

The Metropolitan Museum of Art plans to bring together a collection of some of the world's great pieces of art. Each of the selections will be photographed, made into slides, and sent to schools around the United States to help develop an appreciation and an awareness of art. The museum staff would like the collection to include all forms of art: paintings, sculpture, architecture, design, and so on. They want the pieces to represent all of the major artists and periods of art. To achieve a complete picture of what American students consider important, they are asking thousands of young people like yourselves to help them decide on the most authentic and important selections.

You and your buddy have been selected to do an in-depth study of art and create a list of 10-20 pieces of art that should be included in the final display. To justify your selections, you and your buddy should write a brief paragraph to accompany each of your choices. For instance, you might state why the example is considered art, its medium, and the artist's use of color, style, purpose, or idea expressed. You might also include the reasons why you both think it should be considered. You might tell about the artist, sculptor, or architect and the period in which his/her most famous work was done. If possible, include a picture copy or a sample of the piece you have selected. Please give serious thought to your choices. The slide presentation will give you the opportunity to experience the arts, something you might not otherwise get to do.

## CRITERIA

Research skills

Artistic selections

Justifications

Cooperative efforts

# "Experiencing Art" Bonding Cycle
*Teaching Suggestions*

This activity will be new to many students but will give you the opportunity to bring the arts into the lives of many students who would otherwise not have the chance to see the works of great artists.

Begin with a discussion of art. Ask students to define art and to suggest artistic things. Depending on your two classes, either lead the discussion into the various types of art or list suggestions on the board. These should include paintings, sculpture, folk art, quilting, architecture, and so on. Select books with many pictures suggesting the many types of art from the past and the present and allow several sessions for students to look at them together. These books are available at any local library. As students find examples that they think are worth being seen by people everywhere, they should complete the Extension Activity Form to explain why they have chosen that work of art. If you find that a buddy pair is particularly interested in one form of art, they should be free to select from just that topic, but if they lack a background in art, they need to choose from many forms so that they gain an overall understanding of people's aesthetic contributions.

Encourage students to write to various museums and other places where some of the artwork can be seen. They can ask for pictures of particular pieces that they consider important. Local museums might also have brochures that they would be willing to give to the students; and, of course, a field trip to the museum after the rubric has been handed out would be the icing on the cake. During the tour, perhaps guided by a docent, the various types of art can be pointed out, and students can see firsthand the beauty of the objects and the many different styles that artists have used. Many of the larger museums have slide presentations specifically designed for students that can be borrowed for a small fee. It's worth checking into.

If none of the above suggestions is possible, students can sketch their choices and bind these into a book with their Extension Activity Forms. The real value of this activity is that they will be able to discuss art and share ideas together.

Analysis and Reflection: "Experiencing Art" Bonding Cycle

**STANDARDS: The levels at which students perform the task**

| In Progress | Basic | Proficient | Advanced | Comments |
|---|---|---|---|---|
| Purpose of selecting pieces of art is not achieved. | Purpose of selecting pieces of art is achieved. | Purpose of selecting pieces of art is evident. | Purpose of selecting pieces of art is totally achieved. | |
| Students use only one resource for making selections. | Students use limited resources for making selections. | Students use many resources for making selections. | Students use a variety of resources for making selections. | |
| Most of the justifications writing appears to be word-for-word copying from resource. | Much of the justifications writing is original, but some is word-for-word copying. | Most of the justifications writing is original. | All of the justifications writing is original. | |
| No art selections are based on the qualities of art but are just randomly selected. | Art selections are based on a few of the qualities of art. | Art selections are based mostly on the qualities of art. | All art selections are based on the qualities of art. | |
| Justifications are incomplete and/or incorrect. | Justifications are understandable and somewhat detailed. | Justifications are mostly complete, clear, and detailed. | Justifications are logical and sequential. | |
| Justifications are difficult to follow and lack organization. | Order of justifications do not interfere with the meaning. | Justifications are logical and sequential for the most part. | There is evidence of editing, with minimal or no errors in spelling, punctuation, and grammar. | |
| Errors in spelling, punctuation, and grammar interfere with the meaning. | Errors in spelling, punctuation, and grammar do not interfere with the meaning. | There are few errors in spelling, punctuation, and grammar. | Buddies are completely focused on the task. | |
| Buddies are unfocused on the task. | Buddies are able to focus on the task, but talking interferes. | Buddies generally listen, discuss, and plan together. | Buddies consistently listen, discuss, and plan together. | |
| Buddies argue with and do not listen to each other. | Buddies work but without discussing, talking, or planning together. | | | |

**Rubric 7.4**

# "Experiencing Art" Extension Activity Form

Compare and contrast the following attributes:

Color: _____

_____


Style: _____

_____


Size: _____

_____


Purpose: _____

_____


Medium: _____

_____


Brush stroke: _____

_____


Idea expressed: _____

_____


Texture: _____

_____


Paintings that appealed to us: _____

_____


Paintings that did not appeal to us: _____

_____

# "Experiencing Art" Suggested Books

| | |
|---|---|
| *60 Art Projects for Children* | Jeannett Baumgardner |
| *Entertainers: Through the Eyes of Artists* | Wendy Richardson |
| *Make Prints!* | Kim Solga |
| *Prints of the Twentieth Century* | Riva Castleman |
| *Looking at Prints, Drawings, and Watercolors* | Paul Goldman |
| *Native Grace: Prints of the New World* | Graham Arader |
| *Picturing America: Prints* | Gloria Deak |
| *Prints and Their Creators* | Carl Zigrosser |
| *The Cowboy in American Prints* | John Meigs |
| *Printmaking Activities for the Classroom* | Arnel Pattemore |
| *My Paint* | Software; Saddleback, $32.95 |
| *Kid Pix and Kid Pix Coloring Disks* | Software; Broderbund, $49.95 |
| *Platinum Paint and Coloring Disks* | Software; Broderbund, $69.95 |

# CONNECTION

# 8

# Times to Remember

**Time and Cultural Diversity**

Time passes quickly as people engage in their daily survival.
Precious moments are delegated to deep places in the mind,
soon to be forgotten.
As students are actively encouraged to search for special
celebrations and holidays they will not only have a
written record of a year in their lives but also have
the opportunity to see the
cultural diversity of our global community.

# Outcomes of "Times to Remember" Connection

**Students will write words or sayings to accompany both days of the month and explanations of each picture.**

LITERACY

**Students will make decisions in selecting themes and in describing special events of each month.**

PROBLEM SOLVING

**By making calendars students will learn the interdependence of people across the world.**

MATHEMATIC/SCIENTIFIC REASONING

**Students plan, talk, and work together throughout the year as they develop their calendars.**

PERSONAL/SOCIAL

**Students learn shared holidays and an appreciation of cultural diversity.**

LIFELONG LEARNING

**Students learn skills that will be required in future jobs: higher-level thinking, cooperation, and organization.**

EMPLOYABILITY

**Students use their creative talents to develop their themes and draw their illustrations.**

FINE ARTS

**Rubric 8.1**

151

# "Times to Remember" Materials Needed

- **Primary Cycle**
  Calendar
  Paper
  Markers
  Games

- **Intermediate Cycle**
  Books—Holidays and other cultures
  Paper

- **Bonding Cycle**
  Books—Holidays and other cultures
  Paper
  Markers

# "Times to Remember" Primary Cycle
## *Student Task*

## TASK

Everyone has one special day of the year that they look forward to: their birthday. To make everyone's birthday a special event, we will host monthly birthday parties. Here are your responsibilities.

You and several other children will be randomly given the name of a month of the year. You and your committee will be responsible for celebrating the birthdays of children in our classroom during that month. Celebrations will be hosted on the second Friday of each month in the afternoon. You may choose to celebrate these birthdays however you and your committee would like. You will want to keep in mind what you and your committee will be scored on:

- How well you and your partners cooperated with each other
- How well the party was organized
- The creativity of your ideas
- What you did to make the birthday people feel special and important

Some ideas may include making a special card or drawing a picture. A letter of this task is being sent to your parents and gives the month you have been selected to celebrate. You and your committee may provide treats, but no presents are allowed. It's time to organize, using the Planning Worksheet provided with the lesson. Be creative, and let's have fun!

## CRITERIA

Cooperation

Organization

Party

# "Times to Remember" Primary Cycle
## *Teaching Suggestions*

"When do we go to recess?" "How long before lunch?" "How many more days until the field trip?" The questions are endless as primary students try to grasp that abstract concept of time. Seconds, minutes, and hours, days, months, and years—without lots of exposure to the different lengths of time, children normally have difficulty understanding time. Depending on the developmental levels of your students, this unit and task should be fun and interesting and make time a little more understandable.

Learning from the calendar can include (but not be limited to) number recognition and sequential order, names of the days of the week, names of the months of the year and their order, the number of days in a week, month, and even the school year, the seasons, holidays, and special events, to name but a few. Once you set up a calendar bulletin board, you will surely come up with many more ideas. Teacher supply companies carry a variety of different types of calendars ranging from simple tag types to the more elaborate pocket chart. Whichever type you have can be used in teaching calendar skills. For example, if you use a pocket calendar, the students can daily tell what yesterday was, what today's date is, and what tomorrow's date will be, adding the appropriate day tag to its pocket. You especially need a 12-month calendar, the type normally found in your home. This helps young students see the entire month at one time, which month is next, and so on. At the beginning of each month, explain about it being a new month, its name, and its number in sequential order. Students will then be able to say, write, and recognize the date in different ways, for example, May 20, 1994, or 5-20-94. This is a good time to point out the special events of the month (birthdays, school assemblies, field trips, etc.) by writing on the 12-month calendar or posting a note on the large calendar. The students will then be able to see at a glance any special events coming up. This will also curb the many questions of "how many days until . . . ?" Teaching simple calendar skills can be fun, enriching, and educational. Once you begin, more ideas will come to you and the learning will be endless.

Before explaining the task and rubric, consider the makeup of your class and be aware of any students who might not celebrate birthdays because of religious, cultural, or family beliefs. Alternate activities should be planned for these students while others are working on their celebration and while celebrations are taking place. If this is a concern for your class, you may want to consider using alternate wording on the task such as monthly "shining stars," special people of the month, and so on. Before students begin the task, a plan for ensuring that all their birthdays are celebrated may look like this: If you begin the task in January, celebrate September, October, and January birthdays in that month; in February, celebrate November, December, and February birthdays; in March, celebrate June and March birthdays; in April, celebrate July and April birthdays; and in May, celebrate August and May birthdays. Before beginning the task, consider when the task is to be started, how long your school calendar is, and the number of birthdays you may have in any given month. Be organized—have a chart ready so that students can see the name of their birthday month and know when their birthday will be celebrated. You may have to explain why the months are doubled up: summer vacation, starting the task at a different time of the year, only 5 months of school left and there are 12 months in a year, and so on.

Analysis and Reflection: "Times to Remember" Primary Cycle

## STANDARDS: The levels at which students perform the task

| In Progress | Basic | Proficient | Advanced | Comments |
|---|---|---|---|---|
| Student cannot work with partners. | Student can work with partners for short periods of time but needs to have reminders to get back on task. | Student can work with partners. | Student works well with partners. | |
| Student is easily distracted, cannot stay focused, and is argumentative. | | Student is agreeable and stays on task. | Student takes control, shows leadership qualities, and reminds others to stay on task. | |
| Student cannot help organize party and depends on others for directions. | Student can help organize party by adding some suggestions. | Student helps organize party, offers suggestions, and helps gather materials. | Student is the organizer, giving others jobs to do. | |
| Student helps with project for birthday celebration, but final product is done with little care and lacks organization. | Student helps with project for birthday celebration, and final product is organized and presentable. | Student makes suggestions for making celebration a success and making birthday people feel special. | Student offers many suggestions and shows creativity. | |
| Committee needs assistance to finalize celebration. | Committee needs minimal assistance to finalize celebration. | Final product is organized and shows creativity. | Student's suggestions for making birthday people feel special are thoughtful, creative, and unique. | |
| | | Committee ensures that party runs smoothly with everyone's help. | Final product is outstanding. | |
| | | | Committee's plans are creative and original. | |

**Rubric 8.2**

156

# "Times to Remember" Primary Cycle
*Planning Worksheet*

Month of party: _____

Names of group members: _____

_____

_____

What we will do to make the birthday people feel special: _____

_____

_____

Games we will play: _____

_____

_____

If we provide treats, we will bring _____

_____

_____

Other special things we would like to do: _____

_____

_____

Materials, games, or help we may need from our teacher: _____

_____

_____

**Figure 8.1**

# "Times to Remember" Intermediate Cycle
## *Student Task*

## TASK

Holidays are special times that people celebrate. Some holidays are honored across the United States, and others are celebrated only in particular states or regions. Because America is a country of many cultures, the various holidays give us the opportunity to know each other better. By understanding individuals' cultural heritage, we learn to appreciate and celebrate our differences and the many things we have in common.

Your task is to research all holidays and how they are celebrated. You are to put your information into a booklet. Plan to include events for the entire school year. All the information that you find will be used each month as you work with your buddy on the following calendar project.

You can make your booklet original, using the format and organization of your choice, or you can follow the Celebration Form provided with the lesson. The number of holidays and special days that you research is up to you and your teacher. It is important to listen to the radio and watch television for announcements of special occasions. Read newspapers and look for clues in department stores. Perhaps the best source of celebrations that are new to you are friends, neighbors, or classmates who are new to the United States. Ask to interview them. Their explanations will give you a better understanding of the cultural heritage they've brought to America.

## CRITERIA

Booklet

# "Times to Remember" Intermediate Cycle
*Teaching Suggestions*

All students love holidays and celebrations! These special times bring young people and adults together and provide the opportunity for better understanding. As America becomes increasingly multicultural, many new holidays are being celebrated in our country. Recognizing these special days can instill an appreciation of our changing nation. This intermediate activity is a great place to begin.

Starting with the first month of school, encourage students to read about any special days that occur during the month. (Now that many districts across the nation have instituted year-round schooling, this might be any of the 12 months.) If your students are not comfortable with free reading and research, consider using the more concrete Celebration Form, modeling several holidays together. However, if you have students who are quite original, turn them loose to develop their own way to display information. They might want to create a series of paper napkins, place mats, or information cards. Whatever the end result, students should plan on keeping the "set" together for the entire school year. The information will be used in the bonding activity that will be ongoing throughout the year.

Encourage your students to interview as many new citizens as possible and to report back to the rest of the class. These sharing times will show students that even though we have cultural differences, our basic wants, needs, and desires are the same.

# Analysis and Reflection: "Times to Remember" Intermediate Cycle

## STANDARDS: The levels at which students perform the task

| In Progress | Basic | Proficient | Advanced | Comments |
|---|---|---|---|---|
| Booklet's purpose is not achieved, and few holidays are explained. | Booklet has a purpose, and a few holidays are explained. | Booklet has a purpose, and many holidays are explained. | Booklet has a well-defined purpose, with many holidays explained. | |
| Booklet's writing is barely legible. | Booklet's writing is legible. | Booklet is written legibly but may lack margins or titles. | Booklet is neatly written in a legible style with margins and titles. | |
| Errors in spelling, punctuation, and grammar interfere with the meaning. | There are some errors in spelling, punctuation, and grammar that occasionally interfere with the meaning. | Errors in spelling, punctuation, and grammar do not interfere with the meaning. | Errors in spelling, punctuation, and grammar are minimal. | |
| Booklet is incomplete and/or incorrect. | Booklet is understandable, and its order does not interfere with the meaning. | Booklet is detailed, complete, and correct for the most part. | Booklet is well detailed, complete, and correct. | |
| Booklet is difficult to follow and lacks organization. | | Booklet is mostly clear and logical. | Booklet is in a clear, logical, and sequential order. | |
| Booklet is minimal. | Booklet is completed. | Booklet is attractive. | Booklet is attractive in every way. | |
| Illustrations are absent or unrelated to information in the booklet. | Illustrations are adequate. | Illustrations are appropriate. | Illustrations are appropriate and add considerably to the booklet. | |
| Booklet shows no effort. | Booklet shows limited effort. | Booklet shows considerable effort. | Booklet shows extreme effort. | |

**Rubric 8.3**

160

# "Times to Remember" Intermediate Cycle
*Celebration Form*

Name of the celebration: _____

Date of the celebration: _____

Where day is celebrated: _____

Why the day is celebrated:

_____

_____

_____

Customs that occur on this day:

_____

_____

_____

Why I like this day:

_____

_____

_____

Pictures that remind me of this day:

_____

_____

_____

**Figure 8.2**

# "Times to Remember" Bonding Cycle
## *Student Task*

## TASK

Calendars are systems for measuring and recording the passage of time. In ancient times, people relied on nature's timekeepers—the sun, the moon, and the stars—to tell them when to plant and when to harvest. We are luckier! Since early times, calendars have evolved into the beautiful written ones we use today.

The task for you and your buddy is to create a calendar for the year. Before you begin, you need to decide on a theme for your calendar. Are you interested in a certain career, a time in history, a country, or a particular means of transportation? The theme you choose will be carried out through pictures and writings and will give your calendar a focus. After deciding on the theme, begin to make your calendar. Remember to make fairly large squares to accompany each day of the week so that you have enough room to write about exciting events or celebrations. Check a current calendar to be sure that your dates match the correct day of the week. Draw your picture, add words or sayings, and attach the calendar to your thematic picture.

At the end of school, you will have a record of all the year's activities and celebrations to take home and share with your parents. You can then continue your calendar for the months of vacation, thus recording an entire year.

## CRITERIA

Theme

Calendar

Cooperative efforts

# "Times to Remember" Bonding Cycle
## *Teaching Suggestions*

This activity is one that can be done in a variety of ways. If buddies meet daily, the calendar can be filled in daily in as much detail as you would like. Special days might require more time; for instance, on Valentine's Day you might want to include a card-making project. If you want the students to simply write what their own ideas are, then only a few minutes are needed for the activity, and it can precede one of your ongoing activities. It can even be completed in individual classrooms if circumstances prevent meeting together. Two other options are available to you if the students tire of a daily activity. The calendars can be filled in weekly or even monthly. The beauty of this activity is that you can facilitate its use.

As we've stated before, we recommend that all activities be modeled before students are given the task individually, so begin this task by writing with the buddies for the first few weeks. You might want to demonstrate several different ways to write. On one day you might write a personal thought, something that happened at school, or something that you are feeling. Another day might be a holiday, and you would want to write from a historical perspective. Emphasize that because this calendar is one that the students will want to keep to read in later years, they should make it personal.

In most cases, big buddies will need to help little buddies fill in the squares, which can be difficult to write in. This is great, but stress the importance of the younger buddies' expressing their own thoughts, not the older buddies'. If you enlarge the calendar, it will give the students more room to write.

Calendars and theme pictures can be glued to each side of manila folders, which can then be pasted together for the following month. If your budget does not allow for these folders and you can't scrounge up any used ones, then large folded construction paper will work, although it won't be as sturdy.

# Analysis and Reflection: "Times to Remember" Bonding Cycle

## STANDARDS: The levels at which students perform the task

| In Progress | Basic | Proficient | Advanced | Comments |
|---|---|---|---|---|
| Calendar has no theme. There is little or no calendar form. Errors in spelling, punctuation, and grammar interfere with the meaning. Purpose of the calendar is not achieved. Calendar is difficult to follow and lacks organization. Calendar is inadequate. Accuracy of information is questionable. Illustrations are absent or unrelated to the calendar theme. Buddies are unfocused on the task. Buddies do not work together and/or argue. | Calendar has somewhat of a theme. Calendar follows correct form, and errors interfere minimally. Errors in spelling, punctuation, and grammar occasionally interfere with the meaning. Purpose of the calendar is achieved. Calendar is understandable, and the order does not take away from the meaning. Calendar is adequate. There is evidence of accurate information. A few illustrations add to the calendar theme. Buddies are able to complete the project, but talking interferes. Buddies tend to work separately. | Calendar has a theme. Calendar follows correct form with few errors. Errors in spelling, punctuation, and grammar do not interfere with the meaning. Purpose of the calendar is evident. Calendar is clear, and the order is logical and sequential for the most part. Calendar is attractive. Accuracy of information is obvious. Illustrations are present and add to the calendar theme. Buddies are focused on the task the majority of the time. Buddies generally listen, plan, and discuss together. | Calendar has a well-defined theme. Calendar consistently and correctly follows calendar form. There are minimal or no errors in spelling, punctuation, and grammar. Purpose of the calendar is totally achieved. Calendar is very well detailed, complete, and correct. Calendar is appealing in every way. Accuracy of information is total. Illustrations are attractive and add to the calendar theme. Buddies are totally focused on the task. Buddies listen, discuss, and plan in a mannerly way. | |

Rubric 8.4

164

SUNDAY     MONDAY     TUESDAY     WEDNESDAY     THURSDAY     FRIDAY     SATURDAY

# "Times to Remember" Suggested Books

| | |
|---|---|
| *Festivals U.S.A.* | Robert Eugen Meyer |
| *Special Plays for Special Days* | Mildred Hark |
| *The Holiday Book* | Karen Saulnier |
| *Halloween* | Bob Reese |
| *Easter* | Bob Reese |
| *Saint Patrick's Day* | Bob Reese |
| *Arbor Day* | Bob Reese |
| *Groundhog Day* | Sharon Sigmun Shebar |
| *Presidents' Day* | Jack Winder |
| *Creative Plays for Every School Month* | Ruth Birdsall |
| *The Book of Festivals* | Dorothy Spicer |
| *The Children's Almanac of Books and Holidays* | Helen Dean Fish |
| *Special Stories for Special Days* | Phyllis Fenner |
| *Every Day's a Holiday* | Ruth Hutchison |
| *The First Book of Holidays* | Bernice Burnett |
| *Seasons and Special Days* | Software; Sunburst, $65.00 |
| *More Special Days* | Software; Sunburst, $65.00 |

# CONNECTION

# 9

# Into the Future by Way of the Past

**Bonds to the Future**

By studying the past, people have a historical
perspective to help them discover their future.
By having an appreciation for the contributions
of our global community,
they are able to apply principles that
lead to active, responsible citizenship
in any place they live.

# Outcomes of "Into the Future by Way of the Past" Connection

Students use reading skills to research the history of America. They use writing skills to relay their information to others.

**LITERACY**

Students plan meals, decide important issues for government, and determine displays to be included in a museum.

**PROBLEM SOLVING**

By studying America's past, the settlement of its land, and the development of its government, students see the importance of being responsible citizens.

**MATHEMATIC/SCIENTIFIC REASONING**

Students interact with parents, peers, and buddies in decision making.

**PERSONAL/SOCIAL**

Students have the opportunity to build upon the past to create the future.

**LIFELONG LEARNING**

Students use their creative skills by creating museum displays and reproductions.

**FINE ARTS**

Students see opportunities for employment and education.

**EMPLOYABILITY**

**Rubric 9.1**

# "Into Future by Way of Past" Materials Needed

- **Primary Cycle**

  Paper and pencil

  Various foods for the feast

- **Intermediate Cycle**

  Books—Government

  Chart paper or tag board

- **Bonding Cycle**

  Books—Pioneers

  Materials suggested by students

# "Into Future by Way of Past" Primary Cycle
*Student Task*

## TASK

Many years ago, the Pilgrims and the Indians came together to share a feast. It is still celebrated—you know it as Thanksgiving.

You have the opportunity to thank the parent volunteers who have worked with us in our classroom by planning a feast. Choose either the Pilgrim group or the Indian group to work with. Decide what you will bring to the feast, write invitations, and plan your costume by using what you've learned from the unit.

## CRITERIA

Cooperation in a group

Costume

Invitation

# "Into Future by Way of Past" Primary Cycle
## *Teaching Suggestions*

This unit involves exposing students to a bit of history. Plan a study of the Pilgrims and Indians. Gather books, pictures, artifacts if available, guest speakers, videos, and/or filmstrips to make the study as true to life as possible. During this study, point out to the students the types of food grown and eaten, clothing worn, types of shelter, and the lifestyle these people had. If there is a museum in the area, arrange a field trip. As much exposure as possible during this unit helps prepare the students for the bonding activity.

Analysis and Reflection: "Into Future by Way of Past" Primary Cycle

## STANDARDS: The levels at which students perform the task

| In Progress | Basic | Proficient | Advanced | Comments |
|---|---|---|---|---|
| Student is unable to cooperate with others in the group. | Invitation is written, but student needs assistance to complete it. | Student is able to co-operate with others in the group. | Student exhibits mature ability to cooperate with the group. | |
| Student fidgets, is easily distracted, and is argumentative. | Student contributes to the feast, but success is not dependent on help. | Student displays responsibility, accepts others' ideas, and is supportive. | Student takes control of the group, supports others' suggestions, and reminds others to cooperate. | |
| No attempt is made to design a costume, and no costume is worn to the feast. | | Student designs and wears a costume to the feast. | Student designs and wears an original and creative costume to the feast. | |
| No invitation is written. | | Invitation is written with little assistance needed to complete it. | Invitation is written with no assistance needed. | |
| Little or no help with feast is evident. | | Feast is successful because of student's assistance. | Feast is a success because of student's ability to organize and follow through with plans. | |
| Student can cooperate with others in the group to some degree. | | | | |
| Student is somewhat distracted, needs reminders, and can be argumentative. | | | | |
| Little effort is made to design a costume, and student wears part of a costume to the feast. | | | | |

**Rubric 9.2**

172

# "Into Future by Way of Past" Intermediate Cycle
## *Student Task*

## TASK

A constitution is a set of rules that governs a country. As pioneers moved west to settle new territories in the growing New World, some left the laws of the United States Constitution behind. Yet the people in the growing communities felt they must have laws to live by in their new homes.

Your task is to pretend that you are on a committee of four settlers who have met to create a constitution for your new community. You need to begin by giving your new territory a name. Then you have to decide what types of people have settled there, what their needs are, and what they feel is important to live in a safe society.

Before you begin to write your constitution, you need to study the United States Constitution. It is important to note the leadership, the powers of that leadership, the rights of the people as found in the Bill of Rights, the way to change the Constitution as found in the Amendments, and the reason for writing the Constitution, which can be found in its Preamble.

As you learn the elements of our own set of governing rules, you will be able to decide on the laws that you wish to create for your community. Use the set of questions provided on the Constitution Sheet to guide your reading and thinking. Make your decisions as a group. Remember, this will be a long-lasting document, so put forth your best efforts!

## CRITERIA

Content of the constitution

Cooperative efforts of the group

Oral presentation

# "Into Future by Way of Past" Intermediate Cycle
## *Teaching Suggestions*

Begin this project by encouraging students to talk about rules and laws that affect their lives. Bring into the discussion the effect these rules/laws have on the students, why we have them, and what would happen without them. Then move on to students' knowledge of our federal government and our Constitution. To provide a common background, suggest that students read from a social studies book or show them a video on our process of governing. (This activity naturally follows a study of the American Revolution but can be presented at any grade level to make students aware of the Constitution and challenge them to become aware of what government means to them.)

Once students have a common background, divide them into groups of 3 or 4 and present them with the task, the Constitution Sheet, and a copy of the Constitution. Present the situation: settlers in a new territory with no existing laws and no chance of joining the Union in the near future. Encourage the students to base their community on historical fact, such as a mining area, a ranching community, or a group of missionaries. In this way, students must consider the needs of the people.

Encourage students to visit local history museums, attend a city council meeting, invite a council person to talk to the classroom, write to the League of Women Voters, and read the newspapers for the latest congressional voting. All of these activities will make the experience of creating a constitution a real one.

Give the students ample time to read, discuss, and write. They should use the computer for their final papers and send copies to local government officials and museums. Remind them to include a letter explaining the circumstances for writing their constitution and what the experience has done to make them aware of the United States Constitution. Keep copies for yourself as they will make excellent benchmarks when you use the activity a second time.

Because much energy will be expended on this activity, students should present their constitutions orally. Parents could be invited, and charts or graphs could be made to give overviews. If there are presentations that are particularly outstanding, the school board or city council might want students to present these at a future meeting.

Analysis and Reflection: "Into Future by Way of Past"
Intermediate Cycle—Constitution Writing

## STANDARDS: The levels at which students perform the task

| In Progress | Basic | Proficient | Advanced | Comments |
|---|---|---|---|---|
| There is little or no evidence of study of the U.S. Constitution. Major elements of the U.S. Constitution are missing. Rules/laws set forth are incomplete and lack organization. The new constitution is not relevant for the people for whom it is written. Effort is minimal. Errors in spelling, punctuation, and grammar interfere with the meaning. The group has difficulty staying focused on the task. Students do not listen to each other and/or argue, each doing his/her own task. Illustrations/charts are absent or unrelated. | The constitution shows some study of the U.S. Constitution. Some of the major elements of the U.S. Constitution are included. Rules/laws are adequate but do not follow a logical sequence. Individual laws/rules do not particularly apply to the people for whom it is written. The project is interesting and shows some effort. Some errors in spelling, punctuation, and grammar do not interfere with the meaning. Students contribute some ideas, but one student has more input than the others. Part of the task is done without planning for or discussion of the whole project. Some illustrations or charts enhance the meaning. | Study of the U.S. Constitution is evident in the new constitution. The majority of the major elements of the U.S. Constitution are included. Rules/laws set forth are detailed and correct. The sequence is logical for the most part. The new constitution is accurate for the people for whom it is written. The project is appealing. There are few errors in spelling, punctuation, and grammar. All students contribute ideas to the project. Students are able to stay focused for the majority of the project. Illustrations and charts enhance the project. | Study of the U.S. Constitution is obvious in the new constitution. The major elements of the U.S. Constitution are included. Rules/laws set forth are viable and presented in a logical order. The new constitution is relevant for the people for whom it is written. There are minimal or no errors in spelling, punctuation, and grammar. Group is able to stay totally focused on the task. All students listen, discuss, and plan in a cooperative manner for the entire project. Illustrations/graphs/charts are totally appropriate and self-explanatory and add to the project. | |

**Rubric 9.3**

175

Analysis and Reflection: "Into Future by Way of Past"
Intermediate Cycle—Oral Presentation of Constitution

| | STANDARDS: The levels at which students perform the task | | | |
|---|---|---|---|---|
| In Progress | Basic | Proficient | Advanced | Comments |
| Oral presentation is read word-for-word from the written page. There is little evidence of preparation, organization, and practice. Delivery is awkward. Little or no eye contact is made. Voice quality lacks expression and is difficult to hear. Questions from the audience are not answered. Student as a listener is unable to sit quietly or focus on the speaker. Hand movement is observed that distracts from listening. Questions student asks are inappropriate. | Oral presentation may be read but is made interesting. There is some evidence of preparation, organization, and practice. Eye contact is periodically made. Speaker can be heard by the audience. Questions from the audience are responded to but not always answered clearly. Student as a listener is somewhat distracted but focuses on speaker for the most part. Nonverbal responses are limited. Few or no questions are asked. | Oral presentation is delivered in an interesting way. There is evidence of preparation, organization, and interest in topic. Delivery is engaging, and sentence structure is correct. Eye contact is established but not maintained throughout delivery. Speaker uses a clear expressive voice. Questions are clearly answered. Student remains quiet for the most part and focuses on the speaker. Responses show understanding. Questions asked are appropriate and show understanding of the topic. | Oral presentation is delivered in an interesting way. There is evidence of preparation, organization, and interest enthusiasm. Delivery is engaging, and sentence structure is consistently correct. Speaker maintains eye contact. Speaker uses an expressive voice. Questions are answered with specific and correct information and well-elaborated details. Student remains quiet and stays focused on the speaker. Nonverbal responses are appropriate. Student asks knowledgeable questions of the speaker. | |

**Rubric 9.4**

# "Into Future by Way of Past" Intermediate Cycle
## *Constitution Sheet*

These questions can guide your reading, thinking, and discussions:

Why are you writing this constitution?

Who will be the leaders of your new community?

What will the powers and duties of the leadership be?

What will the qualifications of these leaders need to be?

For how long will these leaders serve?

Can the leadership be removed from their positions? If so, how?

What will be the rules for your new community?

Can these rules be changed or amended? If so, how?

What are the rights of the average citizen of your community?

# "Into Future by Way of Past" Intermediate Cycle
## Constitution of the United States

### PREAMBLE

"We the People of the United States, in order to form a more perfect union, establish justice, insure domestic tranquillity, provide for the common defense, promote the general welfare, and secure the blessings of liberty to ourselves and our posterity, do ordain and establish this Constitution for the United States of America."

1. **The Constitution gives the power of making laws to Congress. Congress shall consist of two houses, a Senate and a House of Representatives.**

### The House of Representatives

Term of members is two years.

A member must be at least 25 years old, a citizen of the United States for seven years, and an inhabitant of the state in which he or she is elected. Representation and direct taxes are decided according to the number of people living in each state. Originally persons not free (meaning Negro slaves) counted as three fifths of free persons for those purposes, but since enactment of the 14th Amendment this is no longer the case.

There can be no more than one representative for every 30,000 people.

The House shall choose its Speaker and other officers at the beginning of each two-year term.

### The Senate

Term of senators is six years (one in every three senators completes his or her term every two years).

A senator must be at least 30 years, a citizen of the United States for nine years, and an inhabitant of the state in which he or she is elected.

The Vice President of the United States is president of the Senate but votes only when there is a tie.

### *Privileges or Rights of Congress*

Members cannot be arrested when attending sessions or going to or returning home. Members cannot be questioned in any other place for any speech or debate in either the House or the Senate.

### *Lawmaking*

Money bills start in the House and then must be approved by the Senate.

When a bill passes both the House and the Senate it goes to the president for approval. If he signs the bill it becomes a law. If he does not want to sign it, he can return it to Congress, which can pass it over his veto by a two-thirds vote in both houses. If the president does not return the bill in 10 days it becomes a law without his signature, but if Congress has already adjourned and he fails to return it, it is not a law. This procedure (failing to sign a bill when Congress has adjourned) is known as the "pocket veto."

### *Powers of Congress*

To levy and collect taxes

To pay the debts

To establish post offices and postal roads

To issue patents and copyrights

To raise and support armies

To provide for the common defense and general welfare of the United States

To borrow money

To regulate commerce with foreign nations and among the states

To establish uniform rules of naturalization (making people not born in the United States American citizens)

To coin money

To set up lower federal courts

To declare war

To raise and support a navy

To provide for calling out the state militia to carry out the laws of the United States, put down rebellion, and repel invasions

To govern an area not to exceed 10 miles square to become the capital of the United States and to govern forts, arsenals, dockyards, and other "needful buildings"

To admit new states into the Union

To make rules and regulations for the territories of the United States

To make all laws that shall be necessary and proper for executing the foregoing powers

## 2. The Constitution gives the "executive power" to the president.

### The President

Term of the president is four years.

Election is by the electoral college. The person having the greatest number of votes will be president. In case no one has a majority of the electoral votes, then the House of Representatives chooses the president from the top five candidates. The House votes by states, and a majority is needed to elect a president.

A president must be at least 35 years old, be a natural-born citizen of the United States, and have lived in the United States for 14 years.

The vice president acts as president in case the president is removed from office, is unable to carry out his or her duties, or dies in office.

Before entering the office of president, the new president must take an oath, promising to "preserve, protect, and defend the Constitution of the United States."

### Powers of the President

Commander-in-Chief of the army and navy

May pardon people who were punished by the law for something they did against the United States

Can make treaties but needs two thirds of the senators to agree

Appoints public officials, judges for the Supreme Court, and ambassadors with the approval of the Senate

Can require Congress to meet on special occasions

Must faithfully carry out the laws of the United States

### Removal of the President

The president, vice president, and all other officials can be removed from office on impeachment for, and conviction of, treason, bribery, or other major crimes. In an impeachment trial of the president, a two-thirds vote of the Senate is necessary for conviction. No president was ever convicted. Only one, Andrew Johnson, was tried.

## 3. The Constitution gives the power of judging to a Supreme Court and lower courts.

### The Judges

Term of a judge on the Supreme Court is for life.

They shall hold office during good behavior and cannot be dismissed unless they do something that is wrong.

United States courts can hear suits between states, between states and citizens of other states, between citizens of other states, and between a state or citizen and a foreign state or citizens.

They can try cases that arise from matters on the ocean.

All crimes, except impeachment of office holders, shall be tried by jury.

Treason against the United States means making war on the United States or joining the enemies of the United States.

No person shall be convicted of treason unless two witnesses saw that person commit the act or unless that person confesses in court.

## 4. The Constitution does not allow the states

To make a treaty with a foreign country

To issue paper money

To keep contracts from being carried out

To grant titles of nobility

To levy taxes on imports or exports

To keep troops or ships at war in times of peace

To go to war without the approval of Congress

## 5. To change or amend the Constitution, two ways are provided.

Congress, by two-thirds vote, plus three quarters of the state legislatures must approve the amendment before it becomes part of the Constitution.

A convention can be called by two thirds of the states to propose amendments, plus three quarters of the state legislatures must approve the change before it becomes part of the Constitution.

## 6. The Constitution, the laws of the United States, and treaties shall be "the Supreme law of the land" binding every judge in every state.

## 7. No one shall be required to belong to a particular religion in order to hold an office in the United States government.

## Bill of Rights

Congress shall make no law prohibiting freedom of religion, speech, or press and the right of people to assemble peaceably and to petition the government for a hearing on their grievances.

Each state will have the right to maintain its own militia and the right for its people to bear arms.

During peace, no soldiers shall be quartered in any house without the consent of the owners.

People shall be free from unreasonable search or seizure of themselves and their property.

No persons except those in the armed forces during war or great conflict shall be held for a serious crime without indictment by a grand jury. No person need be a witness against him- or herself. No person can be tried twice for the same offense. No person shall be deprived of life, liberty, or property without due process of law. Private property shall not be taken for public use without just compensation.

An accused person shall have the right to a quick public trial by jury and may have counsel for his or her defense.

In any suit involving more than $20, there shall be the right of trial by jury.

There shall be no excessive bail, fines, or cruel and unusual punishment.

The list of certain rights in the Constitution does not deny other rights held by the people.

The states or the people, or both, shall keep all powers not given specifically to the central government by the Constitution.

# "Into Future by Way of Past" Bonding Cycle
## *Student Task*

## TASK

Museums are institutes that preserve original artifacts for study and education. Some museums collect and display fine masterpieces of art, but many others tell the story of people through the relics of past ages.

Your teachers, knowing the value of studying the past, have decided to turn your classroom into a pioneer museum. Not only will you have the thrill of going back in time, but your efforts will also create funds for your special projects.

You and your buddies will tell the story of the westward movement and the pioneering spirit of the people who dared to conquer the unknown vastness of the New World. You will transform your classroom(s) into a replica of pioneer life.

Begin with an in-depth study of this time period, the 1700s-1800s. With your new knowledge you can then select an area of the museum in which you would like to work.

Remember, you want to take your visitors back in time, so whatever you do must be authentic. Visitors should be able to respond with their senses—seeing, feeling, hearing, and smelling pioneer life. When your museum is complete, invite your parents and friends to share in your efforts. Good luck!

## CRITERIA

Content of the museum

# "Into Future by Way of Past" Bonding Cycle
## *Teaching Suggestions*

This unit can be implemented for as long or as short an amount of time as you'd like to give it. The westward movement has been chosen here, but any other period of time or any country's history can be substituted. The unit has many opportunities for integration into any curriculum as the task and learning activities are basically the same. Only the reading would have to be directed to the topic of choice.

Begin by encouraging buddy pairs to read any materials that you can gather on pioneers and the westward movement. Videos would bring the period to life and set an example for the standard you wish to set for your own museum.

Once the students understand the era, present them with the rubric and the task.

Begin a group discussion of the various sections that you have decided should be in your museum. Each group has exciting aspects, so all students should have the opportunity to participate in areas of their choice. The research and study skills are the same for each group, so it really doesn't matter in which area a buddy pair contributes; but if you know of particular talents it is always preferable to steer students in this direction. (A synopsis of each section follows.)

Give the groups time to read and plan together. Generally, students should not begin to create until you are sure that they have set objectives. The Museum Plan Worksheet can be used to ensure that preparation is done.

When plans are finalized, give the students free rein. Stress the standard set by the rubric. If possible, enlarge the rubric and place it in a convenient area for frequent student reference.

Your job is to facilitate and guide your students to see that all of them play a part in the creation of the museum. There are several craft activities that could be used for modeling and demonstration, but turning the students loose to decide what will be in their museum will bring the best results.

To prepare for the "grand opening" of the Pioneer Museum, students will want to have costumes. These can be as simple as an apron or a father's straw hat. A bandanna with a pair of blue jeans will put boys and girls in the pioneer spirit.

Besides having costumes, everyone will want to be part of the museum staff. Docents will lead visitors, ticket takers will handle the money, and ushers will keep the flow of visitors moving. Invitations need to be designed and delivered and the event needs to be publicized throughout the community. Those who will be singing and dancing will be performing throughout the evening, but they should be considered part of the staff.

Use our ideas or your own. Like the students, you should feel free to "let go!"

# Analysis and Reflection: "Into Future by Way of Past" Bonding Cycle

## STANDARDS: The levels at which students perform the task

| In Progress | Basic | Proficient | Advanced | Comments |
|---|---|---|---|---|
| Museum task is not achieved. | Museum task chosen is achieved. | Purpose of the museum task is evident in the presentation. | Museum task is totally achieved. | |
| Museum project is incomplete. | Museum project is complete for the most part. | Museum project is detailed and correct. | Museum project is well detailed, complete, and correct. | |
| The presentation is difficult to follow and lacks organization. | Presentation is understandable, and order does not take away from the significance. | Presentation is clear, and the order is logical and sequential. | Presentation is very clear, logical, and sequential. | |
| Effort is minimal. | Presentation is interesting. | Project is appealing and shows effort. | Project is appealing in every way. | |
| Accuracy of information is questionable. | There is evidence of accuracy of information. | Accuracy of information is obvious. | Presentation shows great effort. | |
| If written, errors in spelling, punctuation, and grammar interfere with the meaning. | If written, errors in spelling, punctuation, and grammar do not take away from the meaning. | There are few errors in spelling, punctuation, and grammar. | Accuracy of information is total. | |
| Buddies are unfocused as they work. | Buddies focus on the task and complete it. | Both buddies contribute ideas to the project, and both work on the presentation. | Minimal or no errors in spelling, punctuation, and grammar are found. | |
| Buddies argue with and do not listen to each other. | Buddies each do a part but with no planning. | Buddies discuss the task, give suggestions, and help achieve the goal they have set. | Both buddies contribute ideas and talents to the project. | |
| | | | Both buddies listen, discuss, and plan in an orderly and polite way. | |

**Rubric 9.5**

185

# "Into Future by Way of Past" Bonding Cycle
*Museum Plan Worksheet*

Name _____     Name _____

Our responsibility in the museum is

_____

_____

What we already know:

_____

_____

What we need to know:

_____

_____

Materials we will need:

_____

_____

Where we will get the materials we need:

_____

_____

Resources for our information:

_____

_____

**Figure 9.1**

# "Into Future by Way of Past" Bonding Cycle
## *Suggested Areas of Study*

## MEANS OF TRAVEL

The opportunities in this area are limitless. Most students will think of the prairie schooner, or covered wagon, but many settlers traveled by keelboat, canoe, rafts, or flatboats. There are several ways to demonstrate these. If your students' parents are willing to help them, a life-size model would be ideal, but measuring the area of a wagon or a flatboat and drawing its outline is an adventure in math that all students will enjoy. Small-scale models made of popsicle sticks, tree limbs, clay, or plaster of paris will keep students involved for hours.

## MAP OF ROUTES

Almost every museum has wall-size maps of the country or time period that is being displayed. These can be made by projecting a transparency drawing on the wall using an overhead projector. Students can add the routes of the pioneers along with pictures that illustrate the landforms along the way. Of course, don't limit your students to only these. They will find things that are completely original.

If a wall is not available, a large map on the floor will accomplish the same effect. A floor map can be three-dimensional if you use plaster of paris for the mountains, rivers, and lakes.

## HOMES

Pioneers lived in log cabins, dugouts, sod houses, and sometimes even caves. As in the study of travel, these can be life-size or replicas. Your space and time will determine how you and your students wish to represent these, although the sight of students carrying out daily chores in a reconstructed area could be very appealing for museum visitors. Don't forget furnishings, as some students might want to display these.

## DAILY TASKS

Many pioneers wove, quilted, and made candles and soap as daily activities. Quilting bees allowed new blankets to be made. Dolls were made from apples or corn husks. Bread was baked daily, and lessons were done by the fireside. Students love to recreate these tasks, always marveling at the time and effort needed to accomplish them.

## FOOD

The pioneers' diet was limited to food they could grow. A sassafras branch could be used as a toothbrush. Corn was ground for food and also given to the animals. For those students who like to cook, this section of the museum is a must. Students can demonstrate bread making, grinding corn for corn cakes, and using the limited herbs and spices that pioneers had. These resulting foods could even be sold for a snack as visitors tour. Turn this section into a science lesson by encouraging students to plant seeds, keep records, and graph the results.

## TOOLS/UTENSILS

Pioneer homes usually consisted of one room with a fireplace. The spider skillet, with legs and a long handle, was the principal means for cooking. Attached to an iron crane, the Dutch oven could swing in and out of the fireplace for convenience. Axes, wooden hammers, and saws were tools employed by pioneers. Students can research this area and either make a display of drawings or recreate items with papier-mâché or plaster of paris.

## FUN AND PLAY

Students who love to act, sing, and dance will love this section of the museum. Students can research the songs and dances of the pioneer era, learn to sing and perform them, and create continual demonstrations for visitors to the museum. A video can be made while the majority of the class learns the activities, and this also can be on display.

## SKITS

The possibilities for miniskits are limited only by the group's imagination. Students can act out the daily life of a family, the trip west, or speeches of note. Allow time for them to practice until they are ready to perform on opening night.

## PUBLICATIONS

Every museum has a library, and yours should be no exception. Talented students can write on the various aspects of the pioneer movements, bind their stories, and sell them for a minimum fee. All parents will want a copy of their child's reference book.

## MUSEUM STAFF

Among those needed to staff the museum are docents to lead visitors through the museum, ticket makers, ticket takers, and ushers.

## CLOTHING

All students in your classroom should be knowledgeable about the pioneers' clothing as they will be dressed in costume for the grand opening of the museum. You might want to select a group of students who approve the choice of the clothing, try to find needed items, and help students get dressed for the opening.

# "Into Future by Way of Past" Bonding Cycle
*Suggested Activities*

## LOOM

A small loom can be made for each child with little difficulty. Ask parents to construct a square or rectangle out of wood, placing nails every half inch on two opposite sides. It is better if the nails do not have heads so that the yarn does not catch on them. Old picture frames can be used if wood is not available. The sides of the loom should be no more than 10 inches long.

When the loom is completed, tie yarn on one end leaving a 2-inch piece hanging free. Wind the yarn around the first nail on the opposite side. Do not loop it on the nail but continue to wind the yarn around the second nail on the original side. Continue winding until you have come to the last nail. Pull the yarn tight and knot the yarn, leaving several inches hanging free. Now take varied colored strips of yarn to go across the threaded loom. These pieces should be 4 to 5 inches longer than the loom. Begin to weave the strips over and under the loom pieces, evening up the ends. Try to develop a pattern of color. When the mat is finished, knot the ends of the loom string with several of the yarn pieces and gently remove the mat from the loom.

## NINE-SQUARE PILLOWS OR QUILT

To make a quilt or individual pillows, collect or ask for scraps of cotton material, needles, and thread. (Even boys will enjoy this project!) Cut heavy cardboard into 3-inch squares to use as templates. Students then select material for nine squares. Encourage them to choose a pattern that is eye appealing. If possible, find and display pictures of quilts as examples. Demonstrate how to use the template, placing it on the material and drawing around the square, making sure that the material is not on the bias when you cut it. Once students have cut out all nine squares, they should then draw a line a quarter inch from each edge. These are the sewing lines and especially help the students make an even stitch. They begin by sewing two squares together, putting the two stitch lines on the outside. Show students how to backstitch to end the seam. A third square is added to the first two, again putting the stitch line on the outside. Students continue this process two more times until there are three strips of three squares each sewn together. Finally, they sew the long strips together following the same procedure until they have nine squares in a pattern. At this point you can do one of two things to finish the squares. If students want to make a pillow to take home, cut a square of material the same size as the squares. Use this as a back. Explain how to put the right sides together, sewing along the seam line. Remind them to leave a space open. Turn the pillow, fill it with polyester or old nylon hose, and use a slip stitch to close the opening. If parents are available to help, ask them to sew the nine squares into a quilt. This can be kept for future demonstration or even auctioned off for a class project. Either way, the students will enjoy seeing their artistry.

## EASY BREAD

2 packages dry yeast

½ cup warm water

1¼ cups buttermilk

2 eggs

5½ cups flour

½ cup margarine

½ cup sugar

2 tsp. baking powder

2 tsp. salt

Dissolve yeast in the water in a large mixing bowl. Add buttermilk, eggs, 2½ cups of the flour, the margarine, sugar, baking powder, and salt. Blend 30 seconds on the low speed of a hand mixer, scraping sides and bottom of the bowl. Stir in the remaining 3 cups of flour. (Dough should remain soft and slightly sticky.) Knead 5 minutes on lightly floured board. Shape as desired. Let rise in a warm place (85°F) until double, about one hour. (Dough is ready to bake if a slight dent remains when touched.) Preheat the oven to 375°. Bake for 20 to 30 minutes. Eat and enjoy!

### COLONIAL GRANOLA

4 cups old-fashioned Quaker Oats (uncooked)

2½ cups shredded coconut

1 cup wheat germ

1 cup walnuts

1 cup sunflower seeds, shelled

1 tsp. nutmeg

1 tbsp. cinnamon

2½ cups honey

Measure all ingredients into a bowl. Stir until the honey coats all dry ingredients. Cook the mixture in a large electric skillet for about 5 minutes, stirring constantly. Allow the granola to cool. Store it in a jar with a tight-fitting lid.

## APPLEHEAD DOLLS

Each student peels an apple and cuts facial features in it. Then the apple is suspended with string and given several days to dry. When it is shriveled, students can use newspaper, wire, and masking tape to add a body. After the body is complete, students can make colonial clothes for the doll. Cotton makes excellent hair, and thin wire can be bent into granny glasses. The results are adorable!

## STENCILS

Students begin by researching wallpaper designs of colonial houses. Stencil paper is used to cut the designs. An X-acto knife works well, but students will need supervision. The stencil is then pinned to fabric and students paint the design with tempera paints, the way wallpaper was once made.

## DIPPED CANDLES

Start with wax melted in a double boiler. A large coffee can in an old pot on a single hot plate will work. (This project needs supervision as the hot wax will burn easily.) Give a small group of students a string. One at a time each dips the string into the wax quickly (leaving it in will melt the wax on the string). The students then form a line. By the time they are ready for the second dip the first wax will have hardened. The students continue to dip quickly until they have a candle of some thickness. When the candles have cooled, challenge students to make candle holders from cereal boxes. These can then be covered with aluminum foil to represent silver candlesticks.

## BRAIDED RUG

Students first cut long strips of material about ¼- to ½-inch wide. Teach them to braid by sewing three strips together at one end and lapping the outside pieces over each other. When strips run out, students can sew others to them and continue braiding. When they've completed a long braid, students can wind the braid into a small mat and use a slip stitch on the underside to keep the mat together. These little rugs make darling hot plates!

## EMBROIDERY

After students have drawn a simple design onto a square of cotton material, teach them an embroidery stitch and encourage them to be creative. Many moms will have the needles and thread to donate to the class.

# "Into the Future by Way of the Past"
# Suggested Books

| | |
|---|---|
| *New Friends in a New Land* | Judith Stamper |
| *Squanto and the First Thanksgiving* | Video recording |
| *The First Thanksgiving* | Jean C. George |
| *Samuel Eaton's Day: A Day in the Life of a Pilgrim* | Kate Waters |
| *The Pilgrims' First Thanksgiving* | Ann McGovern |
| *Friendship's First Thanksgiving* | William Accorsi |
| *Three Young Pilgrims* | Cheryl Harness |
| *Plymouth: Pilgrims' Story of Survival* | Linda Wade |
| *The Story of Squanto: First Friend to the Pilgrims* | Cathy East Dubowski |
| *Squanto* | Feenie Ziner |
| *Squanto: The Indian Who Saved the Pilgrims* | James Rothaus |
| *Oh, What a Thanksgiving* | Steven Kroll |
| *A Guide to Artifacts of Colonial America* | Hume Ivor Noel |
| *The Teddy Bear's Picnic* | Software; England, $79.00 |
| *Yesterday's Explorers* | Software; Orange Cherry, $39.00 |
| *America Moves West* | Software; Orange Cherry, $78.00 |
| *Famous Places* | Software; Orange Cherry, $37.00 |
| *U.S. Constitutional Learning Machine* | Software; Orange Cherry, $78.00 |

# CONNECTION

# 10

# The News Is Everybody's Business

---

## Communication

Writing has become a lost art now that people
have the telephone.
The excitement of racing to
the mailbox in hope of hearing from a
dear friend or family member
is replaced with
the answering machine that takes a message.
History, as well as the individual, loses.

# Outcomes of "The News Is Everybody's Business" Connection

| | | |
|---|---|---|
| Students organize their informa-tion into articles for a newspaper. | Students work together to create one product—*a newspaper.* | Students are introduced to the importance of shared information in a global society. |
| **LITERACY** | **PERSONAL/SOCIAL** | **LIFELONG LEARNING** |
| Students must decide which events are worthy of inclusion in a newspaper. | | Students use creative talents in creating cartoons, ads, and layouts. |
| **PROBLEM SOLVING** | | **FINE ARTS** |
| Students see that news is global and of interest to every community. | Students are exposed to the many job opportunities in the news-paper industry. | Students use the computer to produce their newspaper. |
| **MATHEMATIC/SCIENTIFIC REASONING** | **EMPLOYABILITY** | **TECHNOLOGICAL LITERACY** |

Rubric 10.1

# "The News Business" Materials Needed

- **Primary Cycle**

  Paper

  Writing supplies

  Crayons

- **Intermediate Cycle**

  Books—Newspapers

  Markers

  Camera and film, optional

  Chart paper

- **Bonding Cycle**

  Computers

  Telephones

  Job descriptions

# "The News Business" Primary Cycle
## *Student Task*

## TASK

The local day care center is beginning to prepare its children for next year. As most of these children will be coming to school here next year, the day care center has asked that we prepare a newspaper telling the children about three different areas of our school: classroom activities, playground rules, and special classes such as art, music, computer lab, and PE.

Your assignment is to decide which area of the school you would like to report on. You will be given 15 minutes to observe the area you have chosen. Then you will return to your class and draw a picture of what you observed.

While you are drawing your picture an adult will conduct an interview with you to help gather the information necessary to write your article. Please be prepared to tell who the main people were in the area you observed (teacher's name), where you made your observation, what happened at the area, when this particular activity took place (if it is recess, when is recess, and how many times a day do we have recess?), and why this is an important area of the school for new students to get to know.

## CRITERIA

Accuracy of information

Content of information

Accuracy of picture

# "The News Business" Primary Cycle
## *Teaching Suggestions*

Students learn to read not only by reading but also by writing. Growth in reading and writing is interdependent, as research in language development has shown. Students who are given the opportunity to write tend to show an improvement in their ability to read. Therefore, writing is an important part of a quality reading program at the primary level.

When you model the writing process, you are stressing the connections between sounds/symbols, the conventions of print, directionality (right to left), and, most important, the thinking process of writing words. You are actually showing the students how to take their inner language and write it down.

This modeling can take place in many ways. For example, students can collaborate with you to bring sounds and symbols together and to make decisions regarding the use of print conventions by answering questions you ask, such as the following:

- What letters do you hear in dog?
- How does it start?
- What does it end with?
- What do we need if there is more than one dog?
- Can anyone spell bark?

This is an activity that should be repeated often during the beginning of the school year not only for language stories but also for daily diary entries and classroom news stories.

A daily class news book that students contribute to prepares them for the work they will eventually do with their buddies. Modeling this kind of writing allows you to introduce important vocabulary that will be needed for the community newspaper, such as the 5 Ws (who, what, when, where, and why), headline, and supporting details. A simple way to prepare the students for this experience is to follow a developmental plan.

At the beginning of the year, start with daily sharing, choosing several students to tell about something or to give a sentence that they would like to contribute to the news for the day (e.g., "Tommy lost a tooth," "Today is Monday," etc.). After several weeks, proceed to "listening reporters." Assign four students the weekly job of listening to the sharing time and then deciding what they feel should be written down for the news. These listening reporters will be asked questions such as "Who said that?" and "Where did it happen?" to model the type of questioning needed for a newspaper article. Rotate the four reporters weekly so that everyone in the class has the opportunity to report. Repeat reporters if you feel your students need more experience with this type of reporting. (This activity also exposes students to expressive language exposure.)

The final activity, "home reporters," is helpful for primary students before they are given their task. Here they are assigned a particular day when they are responsible for bringing a news item to school. This can be either something that happened at home that they can verbally share or an article that they found in the newspaper. Inform them that they need to have all pertinent information and be able to respond to anyone's questions. Parents can become involved in this activity by reading aloud an article from the newspaper or helping their child decide what home news is important to share. As the child shares, you might be taking notes to help with the writing of the class news item. Point out the positives—for example, "I heard you say what happened and who was involved. Did you mention where it took place?" This type of modeling helps the students realize that by reporting with the 5 Ws they are giving their audience enough information.

# Analysis and Reflection: "The News Is Everybody's Business" Primary Cycle

## STANDARDS: The levels at which students perform the task

| In Progress | Basic | Proficient | Advanced | Comments |
|---|---|---|---|---|
| Information shared with adult shows no evidence of knowledge of the area. | Information shared with adult shows some evidence of knowledge of the area. | Information shared with adult shows evidence of knowledge of the area. | Information shared with adult shows extensive knowledge of the area. | |
| Details are minimal. | Details help describe the area. | Details are clear and concise. | Many details add to information presented. | |
| Accuracy of information is questionable. | Accuracy of information is understandable. | Accuracy of information is evident. | Information is shared in a clear, logical, and sequential way. | |
| Picture does not show area of study. | Picture shows some of the area of study. | All questions are answered with clarity. | Accuracy of information is exact. | |
| | | Picture shows area of study with some details. | Picture shows accuracy of area with many supporting details. | |

**Rubric 10.2**

# "The News Business" Intermediate Cycle
## *Student Task*

## TASK

Many opportunities for employment exist in the newspaper industry. For those who understand the elements of a good news article, exciting and fulfilling jobs as reporters, editors, and commentators await. To encourage young people into the profession of reporting, the local paper has created a contest for all intermediate students in the area. The paper has agreed to publish the winning entries in a special section of a future Sunday edition. The three categories for which they are seeking articles are local school news, local community news, and editorial comments about issues that concern young people today.

After a study of the newspaper, they have asked you to serve as a reporter for this special edition of the Sunday paper. The staff wants to remind you that news can be observed, researched, or obtained from interviews with people experiencing the news. All of these are acceptable methods of acquiring facts. They also want you to be sure to include the elements of good article writing: who, what, when, where, why, and how; detail; unbiased writing; introduction and conclusions; and accuracy.

When your article is completed, type it on the computer. Be sure to edit your article carefully, as spelling, punctuation, and grammar are important. You are encouraged to take a photograph to accompany the article, draw a picture, or include a graph or chart to make the factual information more understandable.

## CRITERIA

Content of article

Mechanics of written article

Accuracy of information

News article format

# "The News Business" Intermediate Cycle
## *Teaching Suggestions*

If the intermediate students are to take leadership in the production of the newspaper they will produce with their primary buddies, it is essential that they understand the elements of a good news article. This task gives older students the background they need.

Begin by finding out what the students know about the parts of a newspaper. One way to accomplish this is to hand large pieces of paper to groups of 3-4 students, who then write what they know and share that information within the group. Rotate the papers through each group so that students read what others know and add any information that they can. The rotation should continue until each group has its original paper back.

Bring in a news article that demonstrates the 5 Ws (who, what, when, where, and why) and How. Copy the article and distribute one copy to each student. Point out that in an unbiased news article these facts are presented in the first several paragraphs. Discuss how details extend the basic information in the remaining paragraphs of the article. When you feel the students understand the format, give small groups other articles. Encourage them to read together to find the 5 Ws, How, and additional details and then to share their findings with the class.

Follow the beginning lessons with a discussion about headlines. Stress the need for headlines to attract the interest of the reader by using words that imply a double meaning or nuance. Remind students that headlines should be short and also create interest. Hand out newspapers and ask groups to find good examples of headlines that are appealing and imply meaning beyond their literal interpretation.

Introduce editorials by comparing and contrasting the factual, unbiased news article with those that purposefully give opinions. Share examples from the local newspaper to lead into a class discussion of some issue that is important to the students. Then model how these opinions could be written into editorials by writing a group letter to the editor of the local newspaper. This is a popular form of writing, and all students will probably want to write one before a school or community event. It might be wise to assign both an editorial and a factual article.

When students have an understanding of these concepts, hand out the rubric and ask them to decide how they will obtain the data they need. They might need to interview other students or teachers about recent happenings or already established programs. They might need to take notes within the community and neighborhood. Or they might need to do research to find factual information and studies that defend a position they might take in an editorial. Once the background information is collected, then students can begin to write.

Encourage them to peer edit for correct format and for errors in spelling, punctuation, and grammar. Finally, ask that students share their articles or bind them together for classroom reading or inclusion in the library.

# Analysis and Reflection: "The News Is Everybody's Business" Intermediate Cycle

## STANDARDS: The levels at which students perform the task

| In Progress | Basic | Proficient | Advanced | Comments |
|---|---|---|---|---|
| Article shows no evidence of news reporting format.<br>Article does not pertain to school, community, or editorial comments.<br>Article is incomplete or not present.<br>There is no attempt to include the 5 Ws and How.<br>Article is difficult to follow and lacks organization.<br>Details are minimal.<br>Accuracy of information is questionable.<br>Information is obviously biased.<br>Headline is missing or is irrelevant.<br>Errors in spelling, punctuation, and grammar interfere with the meaning.<br>No pictures, photographs, charts, or graphs accompany the article. | Article somewhat follows news reporting format.<br>Article can be connected to school, community, or editorial comments.<br>Some of the 5 Ws and How are included but are scattered throughout the article.<br>Article is understandable, and order of information does not take away from the meaning.<br>Details add some meaning to the information.<br>Accuracy of information is evident.<br>News reported shows evidence of biased reporting.<br>Headline is present but may not attract the interest of the reader.<br>There are some errors in spelling, punctuation, and grammar, but they do not take away from the meaning.<br>A photograph, drawing, chart, or graph may not relate to the information. | Article follows news reporting format for the most part.<br>Articles pertain to school, community, or editorial comments.<br>Article contains the majority of the 5 Ws and How.<br>Article is clear, logical, and mostly in sequential order.<br>Some details add to the information presented.<br>Accuracy of information is evident.<br>Information is unbiased for the most part.<br>Headline attracts the interest of the reader but may not show thought.<br>Article has few errors in spelling, punctuation, and grammar.<br>Photographs, drawings, charts, or graphs add to the article. | Article follows news reporting format.<br>Article pertains to school, community, or editorial comments.<br>The 5 Ws and How introduce the article.<br>Article is clear, logical, and in sequential order.<br>Many details add to the information presented.<br>Accuracy of information is exact.<br>Information for local and community events is presented in an unbiased manner.<br>Headline shows thought and attracts the interest of the reader.<br>There is evidence of editing, with few or no errors in spelling, punctuation, and grammar.<br>Photographs, drawings, graphs, or charts add to the understanding of the article. | |

**Rubric 10.3**

# "The News Business" Bonding Cycle
## *Student Task*

## TASK

In the United States and Canada, there are approximately 1,600 daily and 7,400 weekly newspapers. These businesses employ over 460,000 people. They also bring the community, state, and world affairs into the lives of the readers.

Now that you are familiar with the elements of good writing, it is time for you and your buddy to use your knowledge. You have the opportunity to be part of a newspaper company that will write and produce a newspaper for your school and community. The company will be run by you and provide interesting articles for your family, friends, and neighbors.

Because a newspaper requires the work of many talented people, it is up to you and your buddy to study the job descriptions provided and decide how your special abilities fit the needs of the newspaper company. Each of the positions must be applied for as you would any newspaper job that you might want in the future. Together, study the job descriptions and applications to determine the best job for you. You are expected to work as a pair, both doing the same assignment, so talk together before you make your final decision.

Once you and your buddy have decided on a position for which you wish to apply, fill in the application and include examples of your work. Be prepared to explain your work and tell why you are best for the position. Practice by asking each other questions that you think might be asked of you. When you are ready with the application, samples of work, and answers, set up an appointment with the interview team.

## CRITERIA

Contributions to the newspaper

Cooperative efforts

# "The News Business" Bonding Cycle
## *Teaching Suggestions*

Before beginning this activity, it is important to determine what the students already know about newspapers. Begin by having a discussion with the buddy groups about what is news and how we, the public, know what is happening in our community, state, and world. Then review the sections of a newspaper. For future reference, make lists of the information that the students already possess, what they want to know, and what they hope to learn.

Next, schedule several group periods to read and observe newspapers. The ideal situation is to have the latest edition for every buddy group. If this is an expense that your school cannot provide, save papers several weeks before beginning this activity until you have one entire newspaper for each buddy pair. Once the buddy pairs have studied and read together, bring the groups back together to add to the lists you started earlier. If all the newspaper sections are not identified, have students turn to a particular one and lead a discussion about what is special about that section.

When you are certain that the students are knowledgeable of some of the sections of a newspaper, explain the project. By this time the students should be very excited and have an idea about what they would like to do. Hand out the packets (task, job description, and application) and briefly go over the positions. Stress that only so many buddy pairs can fill each position.

At this point, it is extremely important to remind the older buddies that their little buddies are a vital part of the team. In the excitement of the activity, intermediate students might make decisions without input from the younger member of the team. Both buddies should understand that one of the criteria for grading is how they work as a pair, with both participating, sharing ideas, and making decisions as a team.

Give the buddy pairs time to study the packets, fill in the applications, and provide samples of their work. Time allotted for this step of the project should be enough to encourage the students to think before immediately acting. Remind those who finish early that they may or may not get their first choice of position and that they should have one other position in mind. (It's not unusual for all the boys to want to be sports reporters.)

You need to select the executive editors and the managing editors first. These will probably be your leaders, but some students might surprise you with their acceptance of the challenge to lead. Once these positions have been decided, the students holding them become the interview committee for the remainder of the positions. Encourage buddy pairs to apply for these jobs but defer final announcements until after the committee has reviewed all of the applications and has not only selected the most talented for each position but has also balanced out the positions. If there are some that are not being applied for, the editors need to announce this to the classes and remind students that the other positions are limited.

After decisions have been made, have a big announcement day. Congratulate the students and give them time to plan and discuss what they would like to do for the first publication. Some students might need time to interview those in various classrooms or to attend a particular event. Provide your artists/photographers with cameras and film if available. If not, the students should be given time to interview and attend functions with the reporters. Encourage the students to be creative.

What may at first appear to be mass chaos will be alleviated by your establishing rules for self-control. Each group should then be directed to begin work. Rely on your executive and managing editors to do much of the work for you. It's a scary thought, but once you try it and see that it works, transferring authority can be the difference between success and failure. It also gives you time to move between the groups, observe, and assist. It is recommended, as stated in the introduction, that the buddy groups work in both rooms. It definitely cuts down on the noise level and gives the students more freedom to spread out their materials.

There are several options for the business side of the newspaper. If you want to make the paper a functioning one that pays for itself, encourage students to fill the positions of business managers and circulation and advertising managers. If this is a possibility, students can earn money for the supplies needed for the first publication but will need to have access to a telephone to ask for ads and subscriptions. The business managers will be responsible for the accounts. Circulation managers will need to have access to the neighborhood, which might be accomplished by attending a large school function or asking a local grocery store for permission to sell your papers there.

If the money side of the project is not a possibility, then students can become managers and circulators, handing out the newspapers for free in their neighborhoods and making the community aware of the paper's purpose.

The delight of this particular buddy activity is that it can be as simple or as complex as you want it to be. Opening the business part of the newspaper allows for many math lessons on the keeping of accounts, money, and financing. You might decide to have a monthly paper or to have only one. The response of your students and community is your guide. Once one newspaper has been produced, the community might be willing to support the project, and you will be able to add the business phase as a second part.

Included in this unit are guides that can be used or ignored as you see fit. If you feel a bit overwhelmed by the project, start with these guides until you devise your own and better methods to direct and motivate your students. Take a deep breath, jump in head first, and enjoy the thrill of your students taking control. As stated above, it's scary, but the results are wonderful!

# Analysis and Reflection: "The News Is Everybody's Business" Bonding Cycle

## STANDARDS: The levels at which students perform the task

| In Progress | Basic | Proficient | Advanced | Comments |
|---|---|---|---|---|
| Purpose of the acquired position is not achieved. Finished product is difficult to follow and lacks organization. Finished product minimally follows correct news reporting format. Errors in spelling, punctuation, and grammar interfere with the meaning. Buddies do not cooperate or discuss their shared responsibility. Purpose of the task is not achieved. | Purpose of the acquired position is achieved in the implementation of the task. Finished product is understandable. Finished product has attempted to follow correct news reporting format. There are some errors in spelling, punctuation, and grammar, but they do not interfere with the meaning. Both buddies contribute, but one may do more than the other. Buddies each do a part of the task but have little or no discussion or planning. Purpose of the task is achieved. | Purpose of the acquired position is evident in the implementation of the task. Job implementation is complete and correct for the most part. Finished product follows correct news reporting format. There are few errors in spelling, punctuation, and grammar. Most of the time the responsibility of the task is shared by both buddies. The buddies discuss the assignment, listen to each other, and help each other achieve the task. Purpose of the task is evident. Purpose of the acquired position is totally achieved in the implementation of the task. | Job implementation is totally complete and correct. Finished product consistently follows correct news reporting format. There is strong evidence of editing, with little or no errors in spelling, punctuation, and grammar. Responsibility of the task is shared by the buddies. Buddies complete the assignment in a completely cooperative and mannerly way. Purpose of the project is totally achieved. | |

**Rubric 10.4**

208

# "The News Business" Bonding Cycle
## *Newspaper Job Descriptions*

### Executive Editors (1 Buddy Pair)

Executive editors are in charge of the entire news staff. They serve on the selection committee for job applicants to see that all the jobs are filled. They must coordinate the newspaper's content to include a wide variety of news articles of interest to many readers. Also, they must make final decisions involving reporters, technologists, and artists/illustrators. This is a very important position and requires students who have the ability to analyze writing, have a sense of balance, and are able to work cooperatively with a variety of personalities.

### Managing Editors (2 Buddy Pairs)

Managing editors are in charge of the day-to-day operations of the news staff. They are the executive editors' top assistants, helping reporters with articles, technologists with typing and word processing, and artists/illustrators with ideas to accompany articles. This is also a very important position and requires students who have the ability to motivate, are well organized, and can encourage students in a pleasant manner. Managing editors also must be able to help reporters with editing their articles and so should be good with spelling, punctuation, and grammar.

### Editorial Writers (2 Buddy Pairs)

Editorial writers give the newspaper's opinion on subjects of interest to the readers. These writers must be good at interviewing, collecting data, and presenting opinions in articles and graphs. They also must be able to research facts to back up their opinions in the articles they write. This position requires students who are able to meet people, speak well, form opinions, and stand by those opinions.

### Sports Editors (3 Buddy Pairs)

Sports editors are the writers who cover sporting events. They must be up-to-date on most of the national sports and be aware of the sports happenings across the state and nation. They must also observe local and school events and report on those happenings in a fair and unbiased manner. This position requires students who are able to find results and present those results in interesting articles, charts, and graphs.

## News Artists/Photographers/ Graphic Artists (4 Buddy Pairs)

These students illustrate news stories with drawings, photographs, or computer graphics. They create ads, diagrams, charts, and maps to accompany articles. These positions require artistic talent and an eye for balance.

## Advertising (2 Buddy Pairs)

These people call on businesses to sell ads and then create those ads, showing pictures and prices of the product (clothes, furniture, food, etc.). They also write classified or want ads, which are sent in by students or interested members of the community. Students applying for this position need to have good math skills, be able to interview people, have a sense of correct spelling, punctuation, and grammar, and be able to paraphrase. (Ads must be short as they are normally paid for by the word or line.)

## Technologists (4 Buddy Pairs)

Technologists type the reporters' articles and therefore must be familiar with word processing and able to type with some speed. This position requires perseverance, the ability to work with people in a cooperative manner, and skill in editing for spelling, punctuation, and grammar. This is an extremely important job and requires students with technological interests. They are responsible for the newspaper's presentation to the readers.

## Wire Service Reporters (2 Buddy Pairs)

Wire service reporters read news from around the world. Their reports will come from other newspapers and news magazines and from television and radio reports of the latest and most important news events. Students applying for this position must be able to listen, take notes, summarize, and write in an informative and unbiased manner. They must be willing to spend time outside the classroom to obtain the latest news stories. They also must be flexible in their thinking and willing to forgo one story for a better one.

## Personal Reporters (2 Buddy Pairs)

Personal reporters answer letters asking for advice. Students applying for this position must be sensitive to other people's feelings, have a sense of humor, be willing to give opinions, and research for answers to factual inquiries. They must also decide what is appropriate for a school and community newspaper. Occasionally, these reporters add a crossword puzzle, riddle, or puzzle that will be of interest to readers.

## Local Reporters (4 Buddy Pairs)

Local reporters are responsible for keeping an eye out for interesting events in the school, on the playground, and in the community. This position requires students who are very observant and able to recognize news. They also must know what constitutes a good news article, be able to gather information with notes, write those notes into articles, and gather data by using interviewing skills. These reporters have a very big responsibility because they write the majority of the articles for the paper.

## Cartoonists (2 Buddy Pairs)

Cartoonists draw the comic strips, original cartoons, and, occasionally, political cartoons to accompany editorials. Students applying for this position must have artistic talent and be serious and willing to work hard, sometimes outside the classroom.

THE FOLLOWING JOBS ARE THE RESPONSIBILITY OF ALL STUDENTS

## Circulation

Deliver the newspapers and collect money if the newspapers are being sold.

## Business

Manage the money collected from newspaper sales, be in charge of fund-raising events if the paper is going to be sold, and ask family and friends to advertise in the paper for a fee determined by the group.

## Mechanics

Sort and organize the pages of the paper before distribution.

# "The News Business" Bonding Cycle
## *Application Form*

PLEASE PRINT OR WRITE CLEARLY WHEN FILLING IN THE FOLLOWING BLANKS:

Position for which applying: _____

Date of application: _____

Full names of applicants: _____

_____

_____

We are interested in the position because

_____

_____

The qualities we possess to do the job well are

_____

_____

Other information that would qualify us for this position:

_____

_____

Examples of our work to show our abilities are

_____

_____

Signature: _____ Signature: _____

Approval and Signatures by Executive Editors: _____

**Figure 10.1**

# "The News Business" Bonding Cycle
## *Getting Started*

### Executive Editors

Once you have been selected, both of you will be members of the interview team to choose the remaining staff. With your buddy, discuss the job descriptions of the positions to be filled. Decide on the qualities you will be looking for in the applicants. With the team, review the applications, study the samples of work, interview the students, and make final decisions on those who will fill the positions. Complete the Newspaper Staff Sheet.

Once these positions have been filled, you will need to confer with each group to coordinate what they will be doing in their assigned capacity. Each group should be able to show you its plan of action. If groups are having difficulty, you are expected to help them get started. If you find that several groups of students are writing about similar topics, it is up to you and your buddy to find other ideas for the teams to investigate. Remember, you want the news to cover a wide range of topics that will be of interest to all of your readers.

Finally, you are responsible for making all major decisions that involve the writing of the newspaper. These include encouraging the groups, helping create ideas, solving disputes in a tactful manner, and keeping everyone working. Your duties are many, but both of you were chosen because of your talents and leadership abilities.

### Managing Editors

Once you have been selected, both of you will be members of the interview team to choose the remaining staff. With your buddy, discuss the job descriptions. Decide on the qualities you will be looking for in the applicants. With the team, review the applications, study the samples of work, interview students, and make final decisions on those who will fill the positions. Complete the Newspaper Staff Sheet.

Your main duties are to be in charge of the day-to-day operations of the newspaper. It is your responsibility to carry out the ideas presented by the Executive Editors. These duties might include helping a group edit an article to bring the writing up to the standards of good writing or to see that an article is typed by the technologists. You might need to confer with writers and artists to suggest ideas for coordinating stories with pictures or photographs. It is also your job to see that all students stay on task. You are expected to remind students of the importance of working toward a common goal: the production of the newspaper for the school and community.

## Editorial Writers

You have two basic responsibilities. First, you are responsible for writing the opinions of your school's students. You can begin by brainstorming questions that you would like to ask the student body. These questions can be controversial but should be important to both boys and girls. Everyone has opinions, and it is your assignment to discover what the majority of the students are thinking.

The following are possible questions:

- Should students be required to wear uniforms?
- Should school be extended to 12 months?
- Should foreign languages be required of elementary students?
- Should fast-food establishments be allowed to sell their products in schools?
- Should boys and girls have separate classrooms? Schools?

Once you have collected your data, make an interesting graph or chart of the information and write an article that summarizes your findings. Confer with the cartoonists because they might be able to create a political cartoon to accompany your editorial.

Your second responsibility is to write your own opinions on current events happening around the world that might have an impact on you and your friends as you reach adulthood. You might give your ideas on the following:

- How can we protect our rivers, streams, ponds, and oceans for tomorrow's citizens?
- How can we prevent air pollution?
- How can we help nations to be peaceful?
- Should we lower the voting age?
- Will there be enough food to feed the world's growing population? How will we meet this challenge?

## Sports Editors

Your duties are threefold. First, you are on-the-scene reporters for any sporting events held at your school. These activities might be recess games or large events in which the entire student body participates. You are expected to present these events in a fair and unbiased manner using the form for good writing of news stories.

Second, read current newspapers or magazines for national events that will be of interest to your readers. These events might be the Olympics, major basketball tournaments, the World Series, or the Super Bowl. By reading, you will find up-to-date stories of importance.

Third, interview students who have achieved success in any sports area. If there are teachers, parents, or community members who have made similar accomplishments, create a list of questions to ask these people.

Remember, you need to report on different kinds of sports to meet the interests of all your readers.

Coordinate with the artists to create pictures to accompany your articles.


## News Artists/Photographers/Graphic Artists

Your job is twofold: to take photographs and/or draw pictures, graphs, and charts to accompany articles written by the reporters.

If you have a camera and film, accompany the various writers as they attend events. When interviews are conducted, take pictures of those interviewed. On your own, take pictures of news-making events. These events might be plays, musicals, or special presentations by classes, to name a few. Once the photographs are developed, write brief descriptions that explain the photo and turn these in to the Managing or Executive Editors for possible inclusion in the paper.

Reporters who write unusual articles may come to you to ask for help in creating drawings to accompany the stories. The ideas that you are able to present will enhance the meaning and understanding of the articles.

In addition to your own drawings, selected computer graphics help explain the articles.

Remember, you are not limited to photographs, drawings, and computer graphics. You might also be called on to create graphs, charts, and maps.

Keep your eyes open!

## Technologists

Your job is very important and requires knowledge of the typewriter or computer keyboard and word processing. You are responsible for typing the final copy of the articles written by the news staff. Little buddies will need the assistance of big buddies at various times, so it is important that you work closely together. The availability of computers, typewriters, or word processors determines when and where you and your buddy work, but if none is available, then you are responsible for writing out the articles in your neatest handwriting.

## Wire Service Reporters

You are responsible for worldwide news. You should begin by reading and studying the daily newspaper. It will be necessary for big buddies to read to little buddies and lead the discussion about these events, but little buddies should and must express their ideas about the events. If cable TV is available to you, tune in to CNN. Watching the news will give you ideas about what is important in the world. You need to focus on one event, take notes, read further, and write up your articles in an unbiased manner. If cable is not in your school, bring in a radio. It is also a source of worldwide news. Weekly news magazines are also a source of the latest happenings in the world.

It is important for you to be flexible. You might need to forgo one story for a more important fast-breaking event with more interest to your readers.

Always clear your topics with your editors before you begin to write. They will tell you if the items you have chosen are appropriate for the latest edition.

## Personal Reporters

You are the health doctors, veterinarians, and advice columnists rolled into one. You will answer all of the questions that readers send in to you. As you receive letters, be very sensitive to the feelings of those who have written in for advice. At times, you will need to conduct research or interview experts to find appropriate replies. At other times, you and your buddy will simply discuss the questions and give the answers to the best of your ability. Work carefully. People are depending on you!

## Local Reporters

You are the core members of the news staff and must be alert for news at all times. There might be events happening in individual classrooms, events that the whole school will be participating in, after-school activities, or neighborhood happenings that will be of interest to your readers. You should create and distribute news slips that classes and individual students can use to alert you of happenings around the school.

You need to keep your eyes and ears open, observe these events carefully, take notes, and interview the participants. You should have a notebook and pencil with you at all times. In other words, expect to find news everywhere!

Using your notes, write your articles in the correct format. If there is a drawing or photo that will enhance the article, get in touch with the staff artist, who should read the article and illustrate it. Then share your articles with your editors to see if they should be included in the next edition of the paper.

## Cartoonists

Your job is twofold. First, you are the members of the staff who create the cartoons that always bring pleasure and a smile to your readers. It is your responsibility to create original cartoon characters and adventures for those characters. These should either be in panel form or be single-message cartoons.

Second, you will need to create political cartoons from time to time. These should center around school happenings and your opinions of those events. These are your "picture" editorials.

Remember, everything you do must be suitable for a student population of readers and be in good taste. It is also your responsibility to coordinate with your editors to see what will be approved for the latest edition of the paper.

## Advertising

Your position is twofold. First, you must create ads for products that you think would be of value to the student body and local community. Be creative with your ads. You and your buddy can invent products (a homework machine, an invisible calculator that only you can see, etc.) and then create eye-catching ads to encourage readers to purchase them.

Second, you must help students create personal ads that are limited to 10 words or less. If someone wants to sell something, buy something, or needs help, he or she can advertise in the paper. Students can also send personal messages to other students, teachers, or family members. It is your job to paraphrase those messages and ads in 10 words or less while including all of the pertinent information.

All advertisements should be in good taste and suitable for a school audience. You are expected to monitor these. After you have given your approval, coordinate with your editors to see which ads and messages will be included in the next edition.

# "The News Business" Staff Sheet

| Position | Intermediate Buddy | Primary Buddy | Topic |
|---|---|---|---|
| Managing Editors | 1. _____ <br> 2. _____ | | |
| Editorial Writers | 1. _____ <br> 2. _____ | | |
| Sports Editors | 1. _____ <br> 2. _____ <br> 3. _____ | | |
| News Artists/ Photographers | 1. _____ <br> 2. _____ <br> 3. _____ <br> 4. _____ | | |
| Advertising | 1. _____ <br> 2. _____ | | |
| Technologists | 1. _____ <br> 2. _____ <br> 3. _____ <br> 4. _____ | | |
| Wire Service Reporters | 1. _____ <br> 2. _____ | | |
| Personal Reporters | 1. _____ <br> 2. _____ | | |
| Local Reporters | 1. _____ <br> 2. _____ <br> 3. _____ <br> 4. _____ | | |
| Cartoonists | 1. _____ <br> 2. _____ | | |

# "The News Business" Staff Sheet
# Continued

| Position | Intermediate Buddy | Primary Buddy | Topic |
|---|---|---|---|
| Business | 1. _____ | | _____ |
| | 2. _____ | | _____ |
| | 3. _____ | | _____ |
| | 4. _____ | | _____ |
| Circulation | 1. _____ | | _____ |
| | 2. _____ | | _____ |
| Mechanics | 1. _____ | | _____ |
| | 2. _____ | | _____ |
| | 3. _____ | | _____ |
| | 4. _____ | | _____ |
| Optional Positions | 1. _____ | | _____ |
| | 2. _____ | | _____ |

**Figure 10.2**

# "The News Business" Suggested Books

| | |
|---|---|
| *Writing for Magazines and Newspapers* | Howard Heyn |
| *Some Newspapers and Newspapermen* | Oswald Villard |
| *Pocket Directory of the American Press* | Thomas Lord |
| *Beginner's Guide to Writing Newspapers* | Charlotte Digregorio |
| *Newsman Ned Meets the New Family* | Steven Kroll |
| *Children's Newspaper Maker* | Software; Orange Cherry, $59.00 |
| *Writing Fundamentals* | Software; Orange Cherry, $78.00 |
| *Writing Better Sentences* | Software; Orange Cherry, $78.00 |
| *Vocabulary Builders* | Software; Orange Cherry, $78.00 |
| *Working With Words* | Software; Orange Cherry, $78.00 |
| *The Writing Center* | Software; The Learning Co., $49.95 |
| *The Children's Writing and Publishing Center* | Software; The Learning Co., $34.95 |

# CONNECTION
# 11

## Fit for Fun

**Fitness**

To be fit is to be sound
both physically and mentally.
Being healthy enables people to be successful
in the endeavors they pursue.
Teaching students healthy ways of eating
and exercising puts them
on the road to a productive future.

# Outcomes of "Fit for Fun" Connection

**LITERACY**

Students use research and reading skills to discover good nutrition and exercise.

**LIFELONG LEARNING**

By learning to eat and exercise correctly, students can develop lifelong habits.

**PROBLEM SOLVING**

Students have to plan meals, keep within a budget, and develop exercises that help the body.

**FINE ARTS**

Students can be creative in planning menus and exercise programs.

**EMPLOYABILITY**

Knowing nutritional needs and physical fitness gives students skills for many future job positions.

**PERSONAL/SOCIAL**

Students have the opportunity to read and develop models for healthy lifestyles.

**MATHEMATIC/SCIENTIFIC REASONING**

Students must stay within a budget to provide healthy menus for a week.

**Rubric 11.1**

223

# "Fit for Fun" Materials Needed

- **Primary Cycle**

  Books—Nutrition

  Various foods

  Paper

- **Intermediate Cycle**

  Books—Nutrition

  Paper

  Newspapers

  Grocery ads

  Menus

- **Bonding Cycle**

- **Books—Exercise**

  Fitness

  Sports

  Music, optional

  Chart paper or tag board

  Markers

# "Fit for Fun" Primary Cycle
## *Student Task*

## TASK

You have just completed a unit on the basic food groups, healthy food choices, and alternatives to snack foods. You have had the opportunity to taste different foods and decide for yourself if you like them or dislike them.

Some children *never* have this chance. It may be possible for you to give others the same chance as you have had to try new and interesting foods. The school district is holding a contest and has asked the students in your class to join. The school district is setting aside the month of May for menus created by kids. Their contest asks students to design a healthy, interesting menu that could be served in your school. They can only choose 15 menus because there are only 15 school days in the month of May. So, to be considered, your menu must include healthy foods from the basic food groups, be eye appealing (not all green foods), and be creative and original.

## CRITERIA

Menu

# "Fit for Fun" Primary Cycle
## *Teaching Suggestions*

We are surrounded in our lives by fast-food outlets. With busy schedules, time demands, and little time for family dinners, it is becoming common to "stop and pick something up" for dinner on the way home. A sad result of this adult modeling is that our children are being raised with poor eating and nutrition habits. As educators, we need to help youngsters be more aware of healthy substitutes and alternative eating patterns.

Begin this unit by talking about the major food groups and recommended daily amounts and have current data on calories from fat and so forth if your discussion extends that far. You should provide proof to your students that eating healthy will have long-term effects on their bodies and minds and that consuming empty calories from junk food will in the long run cause their bodies many challenges: weight gain, illness, disease, and so on.

Ask your school nurse, food service representative, or a local nutrition expert to come in and speak with the students. There is so much information available on the topic of health and nutrition and public awareness of the challenging nutrition habits of young people that any hospital should be able to give you names of people who can assist in getting guest speakers to come to your classroom.

Also, tour the local grocery store. You might be amazed that many students never get to shop with their parents. This might be a good time to pick up some different types of foods they may have never seen or tasted, such as mangos and broccoli. Hold a taste-testing party at school. It might surprise the students to know that there are some good-tasting foods that they have never known about. This could spur a discussion at home and may have a positive effect on the food choices some parents may make available to their children. Once you feel the students have had enough exposure to healthy alternatives versus the junk food habit, explain the task and rubric.

Analysis and Reflection: "Fit for Fun" Primary Cycle

| STANDARDS: The levels at which students perform the task | | | | |
|---|---|---|---|---|
| In Progress | Basic | Proficient | Advanced | Comments |
| Product (menu) created reflects no knowledge of basic food groups, and most of the foods chosen are not healthy. | Product (menu) created reflects knowledge of basic food groups, and foods chosen are healthy. | Product (menu) created reflects extensive knowledge of basic food groups, and all foods chosen are healthy. | Foods chosen are not typical choices of young children but show original thinking, planning, and creativity. | |
| Menu has no eye appeal or creativity. | Menu has some eye appeal. | Menu has much eye appeal. | | |
| Product (menu) created reflects limited knowledge of basic food groups, and mostly unhealthy foods are chosen. | Menu is typical of favorite foods most young children would select, with some creativity evident. | | | |
| Menu has little eye appeal and creativity. | | | | |

**Rubric 11.2**

227

# "Fit for Fun" Intermediate Cycle
## *Student Task*

**TASK**

There is no doubt that a diet of junk food and a lifestyle of watching TV can lead to an unhealthy body. Unhealthy bodies are at the root of many of the diseases that cause death in the United States. Fortunately, these diseases are preventable, controllable, or, in some cases, even reversible by making changes in the way we eat and exercise.

Your task is to study what experts say you should eat. Look in cookbooks, health books, articles, or magazines that stress healthy eating styles. Because there have been changes in the recommendations by health experts in the past few years, especially in numbers of calories we get from fat, it is important that you use current data for your research. When you have collected your information, use the Food Pyramid Form to show the number of servings both adults and children need in the following food groups: bread, fruit, vegetables, meat, milk, and fats. Explain what constitutes a serving and suggest sample servings on the Sample Servings Form. Then, using your new knowledge and your pyramid, plan your family's menus for a week, explaining how nutritional needs are being met.

Extend your study by imagining that you are limited in your planning and purchasing to $150 for the week's menu. Determine the costs of the foods that you choose by reading your newspaper's food section or visiting the nearest grocery store. Keep in mind that you must meet nutritional needs while staying within the amount budgeted.

**CRITERIA**

Accuracy of information

Nutritional needs

Pyramid/menu

Budget

# "Fit for Fun" Intermediate Cycle
## *Teaching Suggestions*

Begin this unit by suggesting that your students keep a food log of what they eat in one week. When the logs have been completed, the students can classify each day's food into the major food groups: bread, fruit, vegetables, meat, milk, and fats. Ask them to estimate the number of portions that they have eaten in each of the categories for each day. (Since, at this point, students do not yet know what constitutes a "portion," they might want to designate number or size—a bag of potato chips or a large baked potato.) Allow time for the students to discuss their findings with each other, helping each other identify what was healthy and what was unhealthy.

After the discussion, distribute the rubric and encourage the students to begin researching the major food groups. The Food Pyramid Form can be used to start the investigation. Students first write the number of portions that they should eat in each area and then draw illustrations or cut out pictures to use as examples of these food portions. Stress accuracy, for the Food Pyramid Form will be used in planning healthy menus for the family. The students should also begin recording what they eat during the week.

These completed charts enable students to compare what is healthy to what they have actually eaten during the week. They might be surprised by the results. Once the students have completed the Food Pyramid Form, they should begin to plan a week's menu for their own families. Size, age, gender, and level of activity will differ, so remind students to consider these criteria as they plan. Stress meeting the recommended daily allowances in each of the food groups. Because snack foods are eaten by most families, suggest that the students find healthier substitutions—say, pretzels for potato chips or yogurt for ice cream. Students will also want to study labels to determine portion size and content nutritional value. Under a new law, all packaged and canned foods must now list the amount of fat in a product, a big help when determining healthy foods.

Plan a trip to the local grocery store, where students, with completed menus in hand, can see firsthand the new labels and the fat content of each product they have chosen for their family menu. They can also record the prices of selected foods to determine if their menu and purchases will stay within the $150 budget allowed for the week.

Students should then compile their findings. The Reflection Form can be used to start thinking, or students can make an original plan to use in explaining their new knowledge. Invite family members to share results of the project by listening as the child conducts a personal conference on how he or she hopes the family will benefit from the menu created.

## Analysis and Reflection: "Fit for Fun" Intermediate Cycle

| | STANDARDS: The levels at which students perform the task | | | Comments |
|---|---|---|---|---|
| **In Progress** | **Basic** | **Proficient** | **Advanced** | |
| Little information is presented, and much of it is inaccurate. | Some information is presented with accuracy. | Information is accurate and complete for the most part. | Information is totally complete and accurate. | |
| Examples are inconsistent and/or do not include all of the food groups. | At least one example of each food group is presented. | Some examples of what constitutes a serving are shown in each food group. | Many examples of what constitutes a serving are presented. | |
| Food Pyramid is missing and/or not understandable. | Food Pyramid is acceptable. | Food Pyramid is organized and understandable. | Food Pyramid is totally organized and easily understood. | |
| Menus are created without regard to daily recommended requirements. | At least one example of what constitutes a serving in each food group is shown. | Food Pyramid is illustrated and shows effort. | Food Pyramid is illustrated with examples and shows great effort. | |
| Budget and menus are not coordinated. | Menus meet most of the daily recommended requirements. | Menus show planning, and most of the daily recommended requirements are met. | Menus show planning and meet the daily recommended requirements. | |
| | Costs are within the budget, but daily food needs are not always met. | Costs are within the budget. | Costs are completely within the budget and show creative purchasing. | |

**Rubric 11.3**

# FOOD PYRAMID

Fats, Oils, Sweets
Use Sparingly

Milk, Yogurt, Cheese
2 Servings

Meat, Poultry, Fish,
Beans, Eggs, Nuts
2 Servings

Vegetables
4 Servings

Fruits
3 Servings

Bread, Cereal, Rice, Pasta—9 Servings

About 2,200 Calories a Day Is Sufficient for Boys and Girls

**Figure 11.1**

231

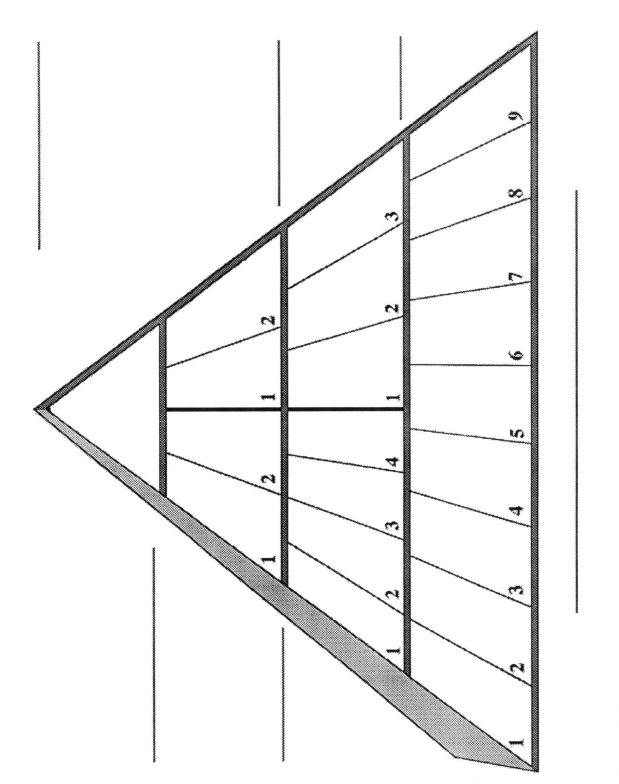

Figure 11.2

## Sample Servings Form

| | | | |
|---|---|---|---|
| Milk Group | | | |
| Meat Group | | | |
| Vegetable Group | | | |
| Fruit Group | | | |
| Bread Group | | | |

**Figure 11.3**

# "Fit for Fun" Intermediate Cycle
## *Reflection Form*

I know that the best foods for my body are

_____

_____

I know that fat

_____

_____

I know the snack foods that I eat are

_____

_____

The most important thing I learned about food was

_____

_____

In the future I will try to eat

_____

_____

Planning a menu is

_____

_____

Staying within a budget is

_____

_____

**Figure 11.4**

# "Fit for Fun" Bonding Cycle
## *Student Task*

## TASK

Exercise is any type of physical activity that uses the muscles of the body. Exercise might be sports, gardening, or doing odd jobs around the house. All of these activities require movements that put the body's muscles to work. Because exercise is important throughout your life, the task for you and your buddy is to research physical fitness activities that will help your body develop properly. Be sure to look for the different types of physical fitness and the effects of each on the body. The categories that you should consider are body building, exercises, aerobics, and isometrics.

After you have collected your information, you and your buddy should develop an exercise program that you can lead for an audience, other members of the school, or adults who come for a family night of exercise and fun. Remember, you have to explain the exercises and then teach all of your program. Both you and your buddy have to play an active role, so it is important that you both be very knowledgeable. You might teach a sport and ask everyone to play, or you might lead a series of exercises that strengthen muscles and/or improve the cardiovascular system. Whatever you decide to do, you and your buddy are expected to develop teaching charts and know the exercises well enough to lead others.

## Criteria

Fitness information

Visual graph(s)

Buddy cooperation

Oral presentation

# "Fit for Fun" Bonding Cycle
*Teaching Suggestions*

The physical education teacher has probably introduced the students to the different kinds of exercises and the value to the body; if not, invite the PE teacher or an aerobics instructor to present and demonstrate some of the exercises to the students. This is a concrete beginning for the research that the buddy pairs will do.

Encourage the students to read and take notes on all the different types of exercise. If they are given the option to pick just one, they will miss the total benefit of the Connection. You might even suggest that students demonstrate one or two exercises from each of the categories.

When you feel that students have researched well enough to decide which exercises they want to demonstrate, suggest that they begin to draw teaching charts that show how to do the exercises and their value to the body. The number of demonstrations by the buddy pairs really depends on the ability level of the students themselves, so they should select what makes them feel comfortable. When students are ready to practice, you might find it better to go to the gym or the schoolyard as the noise and activity level will be above normal!

Encourage the buddy pairs to practice their oral presentations before they actually demonstrate before members of the two classes. Remind them that they should maintain eye contact and speak in a loud enough voice to be heard by all the exercisers. This can be difficult for some of the students and will require practice. As students become efficient in their programs, schedule a day when they lead each other in the exercises they have chosen. This is a good time for them to explain their charts and the effect of the exercise on the muscles of the body. It is important for you to monitor to be sure that the exercises are being done properly and will not harm the students in any way. Finally, prepare for Family Night in the school gym, where parents and friends will be asked to don their exercise clothes and join in for an evening of fun.

If your response to Family Night is greater than expected, you might need to set up a microphone so that little voices are heard. If a stage is available, students can lead from an elevated position so they can all be seen. Display the charts around the gymnasium. Carpet samples, usually donated, will serve as exercise mats. Refreshments can be healthy snacks provided by the students. Even if parents are only able to watch, they will enjoy this evening!

# Analysis and Reflection: "Fit for Fun" Bonding Cycle

## STANDARDS: The levels at which students perform the task

| In Progress | Basic | Proficient | Advanced | Comments |
|---|---|---|---|---|
| Demonstrations are unrelated to any type of exercise and are really just movements. Students are unable to explain the value of the exercise and how it helps the body. There is little or no evidence of research and writing. Charts are incorrect, incomplete, or missing. Buddies are unfocused and talk or play. Demonstrations are awkward and show little or no preparation. | Demonstrations are acceptable but limited. Students can explain some value to the exercises. There is some evidence of research and writing, although limited. Charts are unacceptable. There are some errors in spelling, punctuation, and grammar that occasionally interfere with the meaning. Buddies are able to focus enough to complete the project. One buddy partner does most of the planning and working. Demonstration explanations are read but show interest in the project. There is some evidence of preparation and practice. Eye contact is made periodically and the students can be heard most of the time. Demonstrations are recognized as one of the four types. | Students know the value of the majority of the exercises and can explain their value to the body. There is evidence of reading and research. Charts are clear, logical, and sequential for the most part. Charts are attractive. There is evidence of editing, and errors do not take away from the meaning. Buddies are focused for the majority of the activity. Both buddies work on parts of the task. Demonstrations are explained in an interesting way. There is evidence of practice and preparation. Eye contact is made but not consistently maintained. Students use expressive voices and can be heard by the entire audience. | Demonstrations are clearly recognized as the four types. Students clearly know the value of the exercise to the body and can explain in detail. There is evidence that much research and reading has been done. Charts are clear, logical, and sequential. Charts are totally attractive. Information is correct. There is evidence of editing, with minimal or no errors. Both buddies are completely focused on the task. Both buddies contribute ideas, make charts, and demonstrate exercises. Demonstrations are explained in an engaging way. There is evidence of practice and preparation. Students maintain eye contact and use loud, clear voices. | |

**Rubric 11.4**

237

# "Fit for Fun" Suggested Books

| | |
|---|---|
| *Arnold's Fitness for Kids* | Arnold Schwarzenegger |
| *The Lunch Book* | Kinny Kreisworth |
| *Kevin and the School Nurse* | Marine Davison |
| *Eat Smart: A Guide to Good Health for Kids* | Dale Figtree |
| *Kitchen Fun for Kids: Healthy Recipes* | Michael Jacobson |
| *Healthy Kids for Life* | Charles Kuntzleman |
| *Super Snacks for Kids* | Penny Warner |
| *Bodyworks: The Kids' Guide* | Carol Bershad |
| *Kids in Motion* | Julie Weissman |
| *Make the Team* | Steve Whitlock |
| *Weight and Strength Training* | Ken Sprague |
| *Bake and Taste* | Software; Mindplay® $48.95 |
| *Learn About the Human Body* | Software; Learning Ways, Inc., $79.00 |

# CONNECTION

# 12

# Publishing Company

---

**Theme: Literacy**

Literacy is the link that connects people to the
present, past, and future. The ability to
read, write, speak, and listen
allows people to function in the modern world,
to construct meaning in their personal lives,
and to make both political and social changes
in the world in which they live.

# Outcomes of "Publishing Company" Connection

**LITERACY**

Students will discover the elements of good writing as they help to edit the works of others.

**PERSONAL/SOCIAL**

The ability to interact with authors in making decisions helps students to develop social skills.

**PROBLEM SOLVING**

Students will make decisions about publishing the writings of others.

**LIFELONG LEARNING**

The ability to self-edit is a skill that students will use for a lifetime.

**EMPLOYABILITY**

Good writing skills are needed in almost every job that students will encounter.

**TECHNOLOGICAL LITERACY**

Students will use word processing to make final copies of stories/books.

**FINE ARTS**

Students will use their artistic talents to create illustrations for published stories/books.

**Rubric 12.1**

# "Publishing Company" Materials Needed

- **Primary Cycle**

  Paper and pencil

  Crayons or markers

  Binding materials

- **Intermediate Cycle**

  Books—Fiction

  Paper

  Story map

- **Bonding Cycle**

  Paper

  Markers

  Various binding materials

  Computer program, if word processing used

  Tape recorder, optional

# "Publishing Company" Primary Cycle
## *Student Task*

## TASK

The kindergartners are writing their first books and you have been chosen to help edit and finalize their projects. Using what you know about the stages of developing a book, choose a young student with whom you will work. Remember, this is their book so they should be free to write about whatever they choose. You may help them come up with ideas or extend their ideas, but you may not do all of the thinking for them. Your job is to guide them, write examples for them, edit their work, and show them how to bind their book. They could also illustrate their own stories. You will be scored on your cooperation with the younger student and your ability to follow the bookmaking procedure.

## CRITERIA

Cooperation
Following directions

# "Publishing Company" Primary Cycle
## *Teaching Suggestions*

This unit prepares the primary students for working with their older buddy in the school publishing company. If the younger children are to participate in the jobs of the publishing company they need some exposure as to what is required to write, edit, and bind a book. Working in the classroom with the entire group, with small groups, and with younger students gives them some of the exposure they will need to be a contributing employee of the company.

Start out by turning the students loose to brainstorm ideas for a class book. Choose a topic, and, using the students' ideas, write a story. Demonstrate how to edit the story by rereading, correcting any errors in spelling, punctuation, and grammar, and deleting or adding information. After all corrections have been made either write out the story on large storybook paper or print it out on the computer. Ask for volunteer artists to illustrate the story. Once all illustrations have been completed, bind the book, using any one of the various bookbinding methods available. Students should then try writing a story on their own or with a friend. Encourage them to go through the same steps you modeled: brainstorm, write, edit, put into final copy, and bind. Give assistance to any students who may need it during any step. When you feel the students have had adequate exposure to each of the steps of producing a book, assign the task and explain the rubric.

Analysis and Reflection: "Publishing Company" Primary Cycle

| | In Progress | Basic | Proficient | Advanced | Comments |
|---|---|---|---|---|---|
| **STANDARDS: The levels at which students perform the task** | Student is unable to stay on task or cooperate.<br><br>Student fidgets, is easily distracted, and is argumentative.<br><br>Student displays no knowledge of book-making procedures and must depend on help from others.<br><br>No help is given to younger student. | Student stays on task for short periods of time and cooperates somewhat with younger student.<br><br>Student is somewhat easily distracted, tends to be argumentative, and needs constant reminders.<br><br>Student displays some knowledge of book-making procedures.<br><br>Student can help brainstorm, but assistance is needed with the writing and editing.<br><br>Student can show how to bind the book but needs assistance binding it. | Student stays on task and cooperates with younger student.<br><br>Student keeps younger student on task and is agreeable and supportive.<br><br>Student displays knowledge of bookmaking procedures.<br><br>Student can brainstorm and do writing but needs some assistance with editing.<br><br>Student can help add more to the story by offering suggestions.<br><br>Student can bind book and show how to bind. | Student stays on task and is very cooperative.<br><br>Student shows leadership qualities, takes control, and is very supportive and agreeable.<br><br>Student keeps younger student attentive and interested.<br><br>Student exhibits excellent ability in bookmaking procedures.<br><br>Student brainstorms and webs ideas, does all editing, and helps organize ideas in a logical order.<br><br>Student offers a variety of ways to bind the book. | |

**Rubric 12.2**

244

# "Publishing Company" Intermediate Cycle
## *Student Task*

## TASK

Soon you will become a publisher for the students in your school. Because students from all grade levels will be submitting stories and books, it is important that you know and understand the elements of a good piece of fictional writing. Your task, therefore, is to read as many short stories and books as you can and then practice the art of writing yourself. You need to write several short stories that include characters, setting, problem to be solved, events, and resolution. You need to edit your stories for mistakes in spelling, punctuation, and grammar. Finally, you have to decide if your story makes sense. Is something left out? Are there too many repetitions of words? Do you need more descriptive words? Is the story just not interesting enough to be published? These are questions you should practice on yourself before you begin to help others to make the same decisions.

After you have read many stories (don't forget that *Easy* books contain all the elements of good literature!), then begin your own writing by filling in the Story Map with your ideas. The map is important because this is where you plan. This is where you are sure that you have all the elements of good literature and where you decide what the resolution of your story will be so that it is as strong as your beginning. Finally, learn to peer edit. Having others listen to your story lets you know whether your story is a good one and should be published.

## CRITERIA

Published stories

Ability to edit

# "Publishing Company" Intermediate Cycle
*Teaching Suggestions*

All teachers stress the importance of knowing the elements of good literature: characters, setting, problem to be solved, events, and resolution. Whether students read from a basal or from books, in discussions these elements are emphasized as making a story or a book interesting to the reader. In language arts, the importance of using correct spelling, punctuation, and grammar has been constant throughout the years. All of these teaching skills are embodied in writing and become the basis for the first intermediate activity for this Connection.

Reading an *Easy* book is a good introduction to the elements of good literature. The stories are short, can usually be read in one sitting, and make it easy for students to identify the characters, the setting, the problem to be solved, and the events that lead to the resolution.

It is advisable to model finding these elements using the Story Map before the students proceed individually. Once they are comfortable with the format, encourage them to read on their own. Again, these could be *Easy* books or stories from a basal. Students then fill in the Story Map with the elements of the story or book they have read.

Next, model how some of the elements from the stories read can be used to create an original story map. For instance, students could take the problem from one story, the characters from another, and the resolution from a third. Events could be filled in to move from the problem to the resolution. Once the "new" story map has been created, make a "new" story, with the class using the map as a model for the writing. Repeat this process several times before the students begin on their own. Those who feel really hesitant would benefit from creating a list of characters (monsters, teenagers, parents, etc.), settings (castle, home, hospital, etc.), problems (main character hurt, main character can't make friends, main character has to move, etc.), and resolutions (main character learns to use a wheelchair, main character becomes active on the swim team, main character moves next door to the most popular boy in town, etc.). These lists can be created by the entire class and left on charts for students to see as they write. Remind them that the events should connect the problem and the resolution in a meaningful sequence.

Finally, it's time to write. We have found that you will have trouble getting the students to stop when they feel secure with the process and have ideas that they are encouraged to use.

The process of editing also needs to be modeled. This is best done by asking a student or two to read their stories out loud and then, as a group, making constructive criticisms. Always begin with what the students liked about the story (humorous, paints a picture with descriptive words, exciting, etc.). Next, move to ways that the author might improve the writing or any areas where the listener had difficulty understanding the writer's intent. It is very important to point out that the author has the final say about any suggestions. This gives the author ownership. By the way, if the student has decided to write a book, concentrate on one chapter at a time. Letting a student drone on and on will put everyone to sleep!

Once students are comfortable with the process you have modeled, hand out the rubric and encourage students to begin a portfolio of their own writings. These can be both self-edited and peer edited. The benefits of keeping their writings in a folder are that the students can share them with parents during conferences and can see their own progress throughout the year.

# Analysis and Reflection: "Publishing Company" Intermediate Cycle

## STANDARDS: The levels at which students perform the task

| In Progress | Basic | Proficient | Advanced | Comments |
|---|---|---|---|---|
| Story contains few of the elements of good literature, with few or no details. Story has no resolution. Story has no paragraphs and no transition. There is no evidence of editing for spelling, punctuation, and grammar. Word and sentence usage is unacceptable. Writing is barely legible. Story is difficult to follow and lacks organization. Story is minimal and lacks story sense. When peer editing, student talks and is unable to complete the task. | Story contains most of the elements of good literature, with few supporting details. Story has a resolution, but it may consist of only one or two sentences. Story has paragraphs but no transition. Editing in spelling, punctuation, and grammar leaves some errors that occasionally interfere with the meaning. Word and sentence usage is acceptable. Writing is legible. Writing is understandable, and the order does not interfere with the meaning. Story is interesting and makes sense. When peer editing, student focuses enough to complete the task. | Story contains all the elements of good literature, with some supporting details. Story has a resolution that is partially detailed. Story has paragraphs and uses some transition. Editing for spelling, punctuation, and grammar keeps the story understandable. Word and sentence usage is adequate. Writing is neat and legible but may lack margins or title. Story is clear, logical, and in sequential order for the most part. Story is interesting and has story sense. When peer editing, student may talk but focuses on the task. | Story contains all the elements of good literature, with many supporting details. Story ends with a strong resolution described in detail. Story has paragraphs, with effective use of transition. Editing leaves minimal or no errors in spelling, punctuation, and grammar. Word and sentence usage is good. Story is neatly written in a legible style with margins. Story is clear, logical, and in a sequential order. Story is totally appealing and has complete story sense. When peer editing, student works quietly and is completely focused on the task. | |

**Rubric 12.3**

248

TITLE: AUTHOR:

| CHARACTERS(WHO) | SETTING (WHERE) | TIME (WHEN) | PROBLEM (WHY) |
|---|---|---|---|
| | | | |

BEGINNING

Event 1

Event 2

Event 3

MIDDLE

Event 4

Event 5

Event 6

END

Event 7

Resolution: ( How the problem is solved)

**Figure 12.1**

# "Publishing Company" Bonding Cycle
## *Student Task*

**TASK**

The library is full of books written by many talented authors, but there are many talented authors in your school who need just a little help with editing, writing, binding, and illustrating. This buddy activity will give you the opportunity to help the many students who want to publish their own stories and books.

Your task is to learn all of the positions that constitute a school publishing company. You will learn to interview so that you are able to write "About the Author" pages. You will edit written work, illustrate (if the author wants you to), type the story or book, and, finally, bind it.

Get ready for an adventure in publishing. You will love the experience, and there will be many new books for others to read.

**CRITERIA**

Final product

Cooperative efforts

# "Publishing Company" Bonding Cycle
*Teaching Suggestions*

This activity is one that can encompass everything that is taught in language arts, but it can also be a beginning for teaching students the importance of writing correctly for an audience. It is not necessary that the students have perfect editing skills because they will be learning at the same time they are doing a valuable service for other students in the school. Of course, at the beginning, you will need to hold more individual conferences with the buddy pairs to see that they are making the correct choices in publishing students' work. It is for this reason that you might want to designate those older students that you know are strong in grammar, spelling, and punctuation skills to become editors to help you make some of the final decisions. Little buddies can assume the role of editor with their older buddies. Depending on the abilities of your students, it is probably a good idea to have several buddy pairs act as editors. They can also work in other capacities for other students; it will just take them a little longer because of the interruptions they will experience.

After you have handed out the rubric, it is necessary to explain the process of editing. Not only should students look for errors in spelling and punctuation, but they should also look for errors in grammar. Does the author use a word repetitively when a substitution would sound better? Could adjectives be added to make the writing more descriptive? Regardless of what the buddy pairs think might need refining, they should make no changes without first discussing those ideas with the author. The final decision will be up to the writer.

As student writers from other classes ask for assistance, buddy pairs will need to confer with each student to determine what the author wants from the publishers. The student writer might only want the story/book typed or illustrations drawn. Once these wants have been determined, the "About the Author" Interview Form is filled out. Using the information collected, the buddy pairs then write a short biography for the "About the Author" page that will accompany the book/story in its published form. At this point in the conference, the buddies can go over the writing with the author, determining what the author desires in the size, shape, print, illustrations, and so forth of the final published writing.

With the interview completed, buddies begin their job of finishing the final product. They will be responsible for editing, typing, illustrating, and binding the author's work as he/she has directed. Upon the book's/story's completion, the publishing buddies return the final product to the author.

Providing ongoing lessons in editing, typing, and bookbinding helps the students understand their role in the publishing company. These lessons can be presented to the buddy pairs as a group, with some groups demonstrating to others. By going over the packet provided, students will understand most of the job they are expected to do as a publisher. Much of what you are able to do will depend on what materials and equipment are available in your classroom. If no computers are available, then students will have to write by hand. If there is no binder for use, then students will have to bind by hand or staple the pages. It is not important how sophisticated the process is. Students will benefit from whatever opportunities they are given, and every teacher in the school will appreciate your efforts.

Analysis and Reflection: "Publishing Company" Bonding Cycle

## STANDARDS: The levels at which students perform the task

| In Progress | Basic | Proficient | Advanced | Comments |
|---|---|---|---|---|
| Buddies are unable to work with authors. | Buddies work with authors in an acceptable way. | Buddies work with authors in a cooperative way. | Buddies work with authors in a totally professional way. | |
| Few or none of the publishing elements are included in the finished product. | Finished product contains the majority of the publishing elements. | Finished product has all the publishing elements, some of which are detailed. | Finished product has all the publishing elements, all of which are detailed. | |
| Story/book is unacceptable and must be redone. | Story/book is accurate. | Story/book is attractive. | Story/book is totally appealing. | |
| Illustrations show no effort and/or are unrelated to the story/book. | Illustrations are adequate and relate to the story/book. | Illustrations show effort and relate to the story/book. | Illustrations show great effort and totally relate to the story/book. | |
| Story/book is unbound and/or put together with little care. | Story/book is bound. | Story/book is bound adequately. | Story/book is neatly bound. | |
| Many errors in spelling, punctuation, and grammar interfere with the meaning. | A few errors in spelling, punctuation, and grammar occasionally interfere with the meaning. | There are some errors in spelling, punctuation, and grammar, but they do not interfere with the meaning. | There are minimal or no errors in spelling, punctuation, and grammar. | |
| "About the Author" page is unacceptable. | "About the Author" page is acceptable. | "About the Author" page is interesting. | "About the Author" page is engaging. | |
| | Buddies talk but are able to complete the task. | Buddies are focused on the task but spend some time talking. | Buddies are totally focused on the task. | |
| | Both buddies work but do so independent of each other. | Both buddies work on the project, but the big buddy may do more of the work. | Both buddies work on the project equally and share ideas in discussion. | |
| No discussion occurs between buddies. | Little discussion occurs between buddies. | Some discussion between buddies occurs. | | |

**Rubric 12.4**

253

# "Publishing Company" Expectations

As editors you are expected to read over the story/book of the student author to determine if it is in a form that can be published. If you feel the work is incomplete or incorrect in some manner, you need to hold a conference with the author to explain your concerns. The author will then talk to you about the writing, and together you will decide if more should be written or if parts of the story/book should be changed to make understanding of the work clearer.

After the decision has been made to publish, you need to interview the author using the Interview Form. The information gathered will be used in writing the "About the Author" page. At this time, talk with the author about the size of the book/story, its shape, whether it will be printed or typed on the computer, what illustrations are needed, if any, and how it should be bound.

Once the instructions are clear, you and your buddy need to read the book/story for errors in spelling, punctuation, and grammar. Using a dictionary or Spell Check feature on the computer is essential for all words that you are unclear about. The final decisions can be made by the class editors or by the teacher if there is uncertainty. You then need to follow the author's instructions regarding the cover, binding, type, illustrations, and so on. Remember, in publishing you need to include a title page, the name of your publishing company, where you reside, and the copyright date.

The final instructions are to do your best work. Anything written for an audience should be in correct literary form. This is your job! This is why the author has come to you! If you type, be sure that you leave margins, write titles, and double-space the pages. If you draw illustrations, take your time and cover the entire space set aside for the illustration. If the author wants the story/book in a particular shape, be sure that you cut neatly. In other words, make the publication one that both you and the author will be proud of!

# "Publishing Company"

Publishing Company

Name:

Congratulations! The School Publishing Company is happy to publish your writing for publication.

Someone from the Publishing Company will soon be contacting you to discuss your writing. They will want to know how you want your story or book bound, if you want a particular size or shape, and whether the work will be typed on the computer or handwritten. The publishers will also want to know if you plan to do your own illustrations or whether you will ask someone from the Publishing Company to help you. They will want to ask you about yourself so that they can compose a short biography for the "About the Author" page. It would be quite helpful if you could bring a picture of yourself to the interview. It will be used to ensure that everyone that reads your work will recognize you. The picture will be returned once a copy has been made.

You have many decisions to make before your scheduled interview with a member of the staff. Be thinking and be waiting for an appointment time.

Sincerely,

Your School Publishing Company

# "Publishing Company"

Publishing Company

Date:


Dear          :

We need to find a day and time when we can meet to discuss your writing. The selected time must be acceptable to your teacher and coincide with a time when the Publishing Company is open for business. Please note the times when editors will be available to conduct an interview with you. Check with your teacher to see if any of the stated times are permissible.

Dates:                            Times:

If these times are not convenient for you, please indicate when we can meet by filling out the blank below and returning it to the Publishing Company. Editors will try to make special arrangements for your interview.


Sincerely,



Name:



Date when I am able to meet with an editor:
Time when I am able to meet with an editor:

# "Publishing Company" Interview Form

Title of the writing:

Name of the author:

Grade/Teacher:

Birthday:

Family members:

Favorite subject:

Where born:

Favorite pastime:

Favorite book:

Names of pets:

Favorite sport:

Source of idea for writing:

Writing plans for the future:

Goals for the future:

# "Publishing Company" Publishing Instructions

Title: _____     Date: _____

Author: _____

Teacher/Grade: _____

Publishers: _____

A. Paging and Size: (Please circle the desired size)

Size:                    $9 \times 12$          $4\frac{1}{2} \times 6$          Special Shape

To run the long way                Yes          No

To run the narrow way              Yes          No

Special shape wanted: _____

B. Illustrations: (Please give instructions as to pencil drawings, crayons, markers, computer generated, etc.)

_____

_____

_____

C. Instructions as to type of illustrations: (Please state if a particular picture, graph, or scene is wanted)

_____

_____

_____

D. Cover Design: (Please indicate if you want an illustrated cover or a plain cover that might be made of wallpaper)

_____

_____

_____

E. Binding Choice: (Please indicate if you would like the book bound on the binding machine, stapled, connected with brads or with yarn, or other special means of binding)

_____

_____

_____

F. Special Instructions:

_____

_____

_____

_____

# "Publishing Company" Suggested Books

| | |
|---|---|
| *Making a Book* | Mandy Suhr |
| *Book Publishing Resource Guide* | Marie Kiefer |
| *Book-Write: A Creative Book Making Guide* | Palmer O'Brien |
| *Making a Book* | Ali Mitgutsch |
| *How a Book Is Made* | Carol Greene and Ruth Thomson |
| *From Picture to Picture Book: Storybook Theatre* | Software; Learning Ways, Inc., $129.00 |
| *Mr. Murphy's Chowder* | Software; Learning Ways, Inc., $79.00 |
| *Create a Story* | Software; Orange Cherry, $78.00 |
| *Interactive Reader* | Software; Orange Cherry, $78.00 |
| *Story Maker* | Software; Orange Cherry, $84.00 |
| *The Writing Center* | Software; The Learning Co., $49.95 |
| *The Children's Writing and Publishing Center* | Software; The Learning Co., $34.95 |

# RESOURCES

---

# GENERAL RUBRICS

## PRIMARY RUBRICS

Analysis and Reflection: Primary Cycle—General Rubric for Listening/Reading

| | STANDARDS: The levels at which students perform the task | | | |
|---|---|---|---|---|
| **In Progress** | **Basic** | **Proficient** | **Advanced** | **Comments** |
| Student is restless and squirmy. There is little eye contact with the speaker. Body is not turned toward the speaker. | Student remains quiet, and body is still. Some eye contact is made with the speaker. Body is sometimes turned toward the speaker. | Student remains quiet, and hands and body are still. Eye contact with the speaker is maintained. Body is turned toward the speaker. Comments and questions are evidence of comprehension. Student only listens to own questions/comments. | Student remains quiet, and body is still. Student maintains body and eye contact with the speaker. Student asks appropriate questions/comments and listens to own/others' comments/questions. | Listening |
| Student has difficulty concentrating on reading. Student is easily distracted, or distracts others. Student cannot refocus. Student flips through pages at random. | Student is engaged in reading. Student is somewhat distracted. Student can focus on reading for only a short time. | Student is engaged in reading. Student concentrates for some periods of time. Student may choose to read at other times. | Student is engaged in reading. Student concentrates for lengthy periods of time. Student reads the entire time and chooses to read on his/her own. | Reading |

Analysis and Reflection: Primary Cycle—General Rubric for Writing/Oral Presentation

## STANDARDS: The levels at which students perform the task

| | In Progress | Basic | Proficient | Advanced | Comments |
|---|---|---|---|---|---|
| | Student uses strings of random letters. Words from room are included in string of letters. There is no spacing. | Student uses beginning and ending consonants. Some vowels are used. Student uses a variety of words. Some spaces are used between words. Little punctuation is used. Sentence pattern is repetitive. | Student restates idea several different ways. Standard spelling is evident. Language used paints a picture. Punctuation is evident. | Standard spelling is evident. Ideas are organized. Student uses descriptive language to get point across. Mechanics enhance the meaning. | Writing |
| | Voice is unclear. There is no eye contact. Report is unorganized. Student is unable to answer questions. | Voice is inconsistent. There is occasional eye contact. Student needs visual clues for material. Information is presented in an unorganized way. Student gives minimal responses to questions. | Voice is loud and clear. Eye contact is maintained. Student may use visual clues for material. Body is straight and tall. Student is able to answer some questions from audience. | Voice is loud, clear, and distinct. Eye contact is maintained throughout. Student knows material well. Body posture is straight and tall. Material is presented in an organized way. Student is able to answer questions in detail. | Oral Presentation |

263

# INTERMEDIATE RUBRICS

# Analysis and Reflection: Intermediate Cycle—General Rubric for Reading

## STANDARDS: The levels at which students perform the task

| In Progress | Basic | Proficient | Advanced | Comments |
|---|---|---|---|---|
| Student uses one-to-one correspondence to monitor and then self-correct errors. | Student may read new text word-for-word but shows some evidence of phrasing. | Student uses a variety of strategies when reading. | Student uses a wide variety of skills to decode and comprehend. | |
| Student is beginning to develop vocabulary. | Student self-corrects most errors that interfere with the meaning. | Student recognizes which errors are important to self-correct. | Student makes informed predictions based on prior information. | |
| Student may predict and confirm a word by using beginning and ending letters/sounds. | Student demonstrates understanding through discussion, retelling, and/or extensions. | Student demonstrates understanding of material in a variety of ways. | Student totally comprehends what is read. | |
| Student is beginning to integrate meaning, language, and visual print as cues. | Student can compare or contrast one's own experience with literature. | Student can discuss and retell a story. | Student demonstrates involvement with nuance of books and stories. | |
| Student is beginning to develop fluency with familiar text. | Student makes predictions using book language and story structure. | Student uses expression and inflection when reading aloud. | Retelling is effective and correct. | |
| Support is needed in selecting appropriate reading material. | Student comments on patterns, characters, setting, and plot when given prompts. | Student makes good prediction using prior knowledge. | Student makes generalizations about patterns, characters, setting, plot, genre, and style. | |
| | Student chooses both familiar and new books. | Student makes some generalizations about patterns, characters, setting, plot, and genre. | Student reads fluently with expression. | |
| | Student is moving toward being an independent reader. | Retelling contains some of the elements (characters, setting, event, theme, and resolution). | Student rarely makes mistakes. | |
| | | Student reads fluently most of the time. | Student spends quality time reading. | |
| | | Student makes good use of reading time and often chooses to read. | Student chooses a wide variety of material to read. | |
| | | Student views self as a reader. | Student reads for a variety of purposes. | |
| | | Student usually selects appropriate reading material. | Student welcomes challenges as a reader. | |

# Analysis and Reflection: Intermediate Cycle—General Rubric for Writing

## STANDARDS: The levels at which students perform the task

| In Progress | Basic | Proficient | Advanced | Comments |
|---|---|---|---|---|
| Main idea of the writing is present but details do not support it. | Main idea of the writing is present with a few details to support it. | Writing has a main idea and some supporting details. | Writing has a well-defined main idea with many supporting details. | |
| Writing has no paragraphs and no transition. | Writing has paragraphs but no transition. | Writing has paragraphs and uses some transition. | Writing has paragraphs with effective use of transition. | |
| There is no evidence of following the assigned form. | Some effort has been made to follow the assigned form of writing. | Form of the assigned writing is followed. | Writing consistently and correctly follows the assigned writing form. | |
| Errors in spelling, punctuation, and grammar significantly interfere with the meaning. | There are some errors in spelling, grammar, and punctuation that occasionally interfere with the meaning. | Errors in spelling, punctuation, and grammar do not interfere with the meaning. | There are minimal or no errors in spelling, punctuation, or grammar. | |
| | | | Word and sentence usage is good. | |
| There is no evidence of editing. | There is some evidence of editing. | There is evidence of editing. | There is strong evidence of editing. | |
| Writing is barely legible. | Writing is legible. | Writing is neat and legible but may lack margins or titles. | Writing is neat and style is legible with margins and titles. | |

Analysis and Reflection: Intermediate Cycle—General Rubric for Listening

| | STANDARDS: The levels at which students perform the task | | | |
|---|---|---|---|---|
| **In Progress** | **Basic** | **Proficient** | **Advanced** | **Comments** |
| Student is unable to sit quietly.<br><br>Hand movement that is observed distracts from listening.<br><br>Student is unable to focus on the speaker.<br><br>Questions asked of the speaker are inappropriate. | Student listens to the speaker but may be distracted or use hand movements.<br><br>Student focuses on the speaker most of the time.<br><br>Responses to the speaker may be nonexistent or limited.<br><br>Few or no questions are asked of the speaker. | Student remains quiet for the most part.<br><br>Student focuses on the speaker during the presentation.<br><br>Responses to the speaker show understanding.<br><br>Questions asked are appropriate and show understanding of the topic. | Student remains quiet with still hands throughout the entire presentation.<br><br>Student is focused on the speaker.<br><br>Responses to the speaker are appropriate and show understanding.<br><br>Student asks knowledge-able questions of the speaker. | |

Analysis and Reflection: Intermediate Cycle—General Rubric for Oral Presentation

## STANDARDS: The levels at which students perform the task

| In Progress | Basic | Proficient | Advanced | Comments |
|---|---|---|---|---|
| Information is generally read word-for-word from the written page. | Information may be read but is done so with clear evidence of interest in the report. | Information is presented, rather than read, in an interesting way. | Information is presented rather than read. | |
| There is little, if any, evidence of preparation, organization, or practice for the presentation. | There is some evidence of preparation, organization, and practice for the presentation. | There is evidence of preparation, organization, and interest in the topic. | Presentation is interesting. There is evidence or preparation, organization, and enthusiasm for the topic. | |
| Delivery is awkward. | Eye contact is periodically made. Speaker can be heard by the audience. | Delivery is engaging, and sentence structure is generally correct. | Delivery is engaging. Sentence structure is consistently correct. | |
| There is little or no eye contact with the audience. | | Eye contact is established although not maintained throughout the delivery. | | |
| Voice lacks expression and is difficult to hear. | Questions by the audience are answered, but answers are not always clear. | Speaker uses an expressive voice that can be clearly heard by the audience. | Speaker makes and maintains eye contact and uses an expressive voice that can be heard by the audience. | |
| Questions from the audience are generally not answered. | | Questions from the audience are clearly answered. | Questions from the audience are clearly answered with specific and correct information and detail. | |

269

Analysis and Reflection: Intermediate Cycle—General Rubric for Content

## STANDARDS: The levels at which students perform the task

| In Progress | Basic | Proficient | Advanced | Comments |
|---|---|---|---|---|
| Purpose of the task is not achieved. | Purpose of the project is achieved in the task. | Project is detailed, complete, and correct. | Purpose of the project is totally achieved in the task. | |
| Project is incomplete and/or incorrect. | Project has details and is complete for the most part. | Project is clear, and the order is logical and sequential for the most part. | Project is well detailed, complete, and correct. | |
| Project is difficult to follow and lacks organization. | Project is understandable, and the order of the presentation does not take away from its meaning. | Project presented is clear, logical, and in sequential order. | | |
| Project is minimal. | | Project is appealing. | Project is appealing in every aspect. | |
| Accuracy of information is questionable. | Project is interesting. | Accuracy of information is obvious. | Information is totally accurate. | |
| Errors in grammar, spelling, and punctuation interfere with the meaning. | There is evidence of accuracy of information. | Project has few errors in spelling, punctuation, and grammar. | There is evidence of editing, with minimal or no errors in spelling, punctuation, and grammar. | |
| Illustrations/charts are absent or unrelated. | Project has some errors in spelling, grammar, and punctuation, but they do not distract from the meaning. | Illustrations/charts enhance the project. | Illustrations/charts/graphs are appropriate and add to the project. | |
| | Some illustrations/charts are given to enhance the meaning. Purpose of the project is evident in the task. | | | |

# BONDING RUBRICS

Analysis and Reflection: Bonding Cycle—General Rubric for Bonding Activity

## STANDARDS: The levels at which students perform the task

| In Progress | Basic | Proficient | Advanced | Comments |
|---|---|---|---|---|
| Buddies are unfocused on the task. | Buddies focus on the project and participate in the task. | Buddies are focused on the task for most of the time allotted. | Buddies are completely focused on the task. | |
| Buddies talk loudly or play noisily. | Buddies are working but talking too much. | Buddies work, but talk interferes somewhat with the completion of the task. | Buddies work quietly for the entire shared time. | |
| Buddies do not contribute ideas and talents to the project. | Buddies contribute some ideas, but one of the partners may have more input. | Both buddies contribute ideas to the project, and both work on the task. | Buddies contribute their ideas and their talents to the project. | |
| Buddies do not listen to each other and/or argue with each other. | Buddies each do a part of the task without discussion or planning. | Buddies discuss the project, listen to each other's suggestions, and help each other achieve the task. | Buddies listen, discuss, and plan in a mannerly way. | |

# Bibliography

---

## WHOLE LANGUAGE

Goodman, K. S. (1986). *What's whole in whole language.* Portsmouth, NH: Heinnemann.

Graves, D., & Stuart, V. (1985). *Write from the start.* New York: Signet.

Johnson, T. D., & Louis, D. (1988). *Literacy through literature.* Portsmouth, NH: Heinnemann.

Mills, H., & Cllyde, J. A. (1990). *Portraits of a whole language classroom.* Portsmouth, NH: Heinnemann.

Newman, J. M. (Ed.). (1985). *Whole language theory in use.* Portsmouth, NH: Heinnemann.

Routman, R. (1988). *Transitions: From literature to literacy.* Portsmouth, NH: Heinnemann.

Routman, R. (1991). *Invitations: Changing as teachers and learners.* Portsmouth, NH: Heinnemann.

Stuart-Dore, N. (Ed.). (1986). *Writing and reading to learn.* Rozelle, New South Wales: Australia: Primary English Teaching Association.

Venezkky, R. L., Wagner, D. A., & Ciliberti, B. S. (1990). *Toward defining literacy.* Newark, DE: International Reading Association.

## ASSESSMENT

Bouffler, C. (Ed.). (1993). *Literacy evaluation: Issues and practicalities.* Portsmouth, NH: Heinnemann.

Goodman, K. S., Bird, L. B., & Goodman, Y. (1992). *The whole language catalog: Supplement on authentic assessment.* New York: Macmillan/McGraw-Hill.

IRA/NCTE Joint Task Force on Assessment. (1994). *Standards for the assessment of reading and writing.* Newark, DE: International Reading Association.

Rhodes, L. K. (1992). *Literacy assessment.* Portsmouth, NH: Heinnemann.

Rhodes, L. K., & Shanklin, N. (1992). *Windows into literacy.* Portsmouth, NH: Heinnemann.

Samuels, S. J., & Farstrup, A. E. (Eds.). (1992). Assessing literacy: From standardized to portfolios and performance. In *What research has to say about reading instruction* (pp. 70-100). Newark, DE: International Reading Association.

Valencia, S. W., Hiebert, E. H., & Afflervack, P. P. (Eds.). (1994). *Authentic reading assessment.* Newark, DE: International Reading Association.

## CONSTRUCTIVIST THEORY

Brooks, J. G., & Brooks, M. G. (1993). *The case for constructivist classrooms.* Alexandria, VA: Association for Supervision and Curriculum Development.

Claggett, F., & Brown, J. (1992). *Drawing your own conclusions.* Portsmouth, NH: Heinnemann.

Culligan, B. E. (Ed.). (1987). *Children's literature in the reading program.* Newark, DE: International Reading Association.

Wells, G., & Chang-Wells, G. L. (1992). *Constructing knowledge together.* Portsmouth, NH: Heinnemann.

Zemelman, S., Daniels, H., & Hyde, A. (1993). *Best practice and learning in America's schools.* Portsmouth, NH: Heinnemann.

## THEMATIC UNITS AND HIGHER-LEVEL THINKING

Eggen, P., & Main, J. (1990). *Developing critical thinking through science: Book 2.* Pacific Grove, CA: Critical Thinking Press & Software.

Hart-Heewins, L., & Wells, J. (1992). *Read it in the classroom.* Portsmouth, NH: Heinnemann.

Lipson, M., Valencia, S., Wixson, K. K., & Peters, C. (1993). Integration and thematic teaching: Integration to improve teaching and learning. *Language Arts, 4,* 252-263.

Lowery, F. (1985). *The everyday science sourcebook: Ideas for teaching in the elementary and middle schools.* Menlo Park, CA: Seymour.

Pigdon, K., & Wolley, M. (Eds.). (1993). *The big picture: Integrating children's learning.* Portsmouth, NH: Heinnemann.

Polette, N. (1987). *The ABC's of book and thinking skills.* St. Charles, MO: Book Lures.

Raths, L. E., Wassermann, S., Jonas, A., & Rothstein, A. (1986). *Teaching for thinking: Theory, strategies and activities for the classroom.* New York: Columbia University Press.

Wilson, L. (1993). *An integrated approach to learning.* Portsmouth, NH: Heinnemann.

## CROSS-GRADE-LEVEL TEACHING/PEER TUTORING

Bromley, K. D'A. (1989). Buddy journals make the reading-writing connection. *The Reading Teacher, 43,* 122-129.

Labbon L. D., & Teale, W. H. (1990). Crossage reading: A strategy for helping poor readers. *The Reading Teacher, 44,* 362-369.

Leland, C., & Fitzpatrick, R. (1993). Crossage interaction builds enthusiasm for reading and writing. *The Reading Teacher, 47,* 292-301.

## COOPERATIVE LEARNING

Albert, L. (1989). *A teachers' guide to cooperative discipline: How to manage your classroom and promote self-esteem.* Circle Pines, MN: American Guidance Service.

Johnson, D. W., Johnson, R., & Holubec, E. (1988). *Cooperation in the classroom.* Edina, MN: Interaction Book Company.

Kagan, S. (1988). *Cooperative learning: Resources for teachers.* Riverside: University of California Press.

Slavin, R. (1983). *Cooperative learning.* New York: Longman.

CORWIN
PRESS

**The Corwin Press logo**—a raven striding across an open book—represents the happy union of courage and learning. We are a professional-level publisher of books and journals for K-12 educators, and we are committed to creating and providing resources that embody these qualities. Corwin's motto is "Success for All Learners."